OVERCOMING LOSS AND EMBRACING HOPE

OVERCOMING LOSS AND EMBRACING HOPE

A 9/11 Widow's Story

Kathy Trant

AuthorHouse™
1663 Liberty Drive
Bloomington, IN 47403
www.authorhouse.com
Phone: 1-800-839-8640

Published by AuthorHouse 6/24/2014

ISBN: 978-1-4969-2045-4 (sc)
ISBN: 978-1-4969-2044-7 (hc)
ISBN: 978-1-4969-2043-0 (e)

Library of Congress Control Number: 2014910965

Dedication

My soul mate, Danny Trant
Thank you for teaching me to enjoy life. To me, you were
the most amazing person and the greatest man who has
ever lived. To say I miss you doesn't say enough.

Thank you

Kelly Cahill and Mary Beth Dooley Horsington, thank
you for your assistance in writing and editing this
book. I couldn't have done it without you both.

PROLOGUE

"I love you," he says. Then, the phone goes dead.

We all watched as it happened. Many of us didn't need a television to see it. We all watched as thousands of people awaited death. You could see what looked like confetti falling from the sky, but it was people jumping from the windows of the buildings to their deaths.

People were running from the towers screaming in fear at what was happening. The victims had burned skin, clothes soaked with blood, and terror in their eyes. We were all in total denial.

Was it an accident?

No, it wasn't.

The smoke from the towers began to saturate the air. We were all thinking the same thing – *how many people are still in the buildings?* You could see firefighters, police officers, and other brave souls risking their lives as they returned to the scene to save as many lives as possible. Other New York City residents were standing in the streets shocked by what was happening right before their eyes. All we could do was stop, stare, and pray.

Suddenly, I watched as the towers crumbled to the ground, one, and then the other. I dropped to my knees in despair as I pulled one of my boys to me and held him in my arms.

Families all over the world watched their televisions and sobbed. Many families hovered over the phone in hopes of a call informing them their loved ones made it out alive. Wherever you went, flyers were posted by family and friends searching for their missing loved ones.

Were they alive?

Were they hurt?

Were they dead?

What began as a beautiful, sunny Tuesday morning became a devastating nightmare America will never forget.

INTRODUCTION

Danny was a man of love, murdered by hate. When I lost him, my life shattered into a million painful pieces. To fully understand what an honorable man he was and how profoundly his death affected those who loved him, I want to share my struggle to survive following his tragic death.

I am not perfect, and I have made many serious mistakes. I have hurt others and hurt myself as I battled bipolar disorder, drug addiction, compulsive spending, and PTSD. During my most vulnerable period, I made one of the most serious mistakes of my life – I bared my soul to the public in national newspapers, magazines, and talk shows. The resulting media firestorm nearly destroyed me. I became known as the "Crazy 9/11 Widow."

This is a struggle that remains deeply painful for me, and I have feelings of guilt and shame about it. But my biggest worry is that my actions tarnished my loving husband's memory. By writing about these experiences, my intent is not just to set the record straight so that my actions might be explained, but to share the legacy of my husband. I believe that if people understand my family's battles, they might be able to hear the message I hope to send about Danny.

Other people will also share their feelings about Danny through letters. So many paid tribute to "Dan the Man" after 9/11. For me, those letters are the heart of this book. They keep the focus squarely where it should be: on this very special man named Daniel Trant.

Our daughter, Jessica, tells her father's story from her own perspective. I believe it is a testament to the truth of my relationship with Danny. I can say whatever I like about my marriage to her father, and make any claim at all about how perfect we were together. But Jessica witnessed it firsthand. She saw the love Danny and I had for each other, as well as for her and her brothers.

I fell apart. It has taken me over a decade to put myself back together again, but of course I didn't do it alone. So many of the people in my life helped, along with my trusted therapist.

I want to give heartfelt thanks to the New York City firefighters, policeman, and other first responders who tried to save my husband's life. You are all my heroes. I can never thank you enough. For those who also lost their own lives while trying to save others, I have a hole in my heart forever. I feel the same way about the men and women who serve in our armed forces, fighting to keep our country safe.

Finally, I want to thank all the people who reached out to me after 9/11. I received support from so many people – family, friends, and people I didn't even know. I felt lifted up by people across America and around the world, held in their arms. Without that outpouring of love and support, I honestly believe that I would not be here today. I can't even begin to express the gratitude I feel.

From the bottom of my heart . . .
THANK YOU.

CHAPTER 1

"Nobody can go back and start a new beginning, but anyone can start today and make a new ending."

- Maria Robinson -

I was born in Staten Island, New York, in 1962. I had an older brother and a younger sister, but I was always considered the tough kid – my mother says I was definitely the most difficult child to raise. Strong willed and emotional. Fearful and defiant. A personality filled with contradictions.

My parents divorced when I was 5, and my mother was left alone with three children and no support system. But she was a sunny optimist – she didn't give in to despair. She did the best she could to keep us all afloat, but I know she struggled mightily. I internalized enough anxiety for both of us.

A "rescue" came in the form of a stepfather when I was six. He married my mother and moved us to Connecticut, and then to Massachusetts. I remember riding in my stepfather's old Cadillac, feeling anxious and scared. But mostly, lonely. Loneliness became my constant companion, and it stayed with me throughout my childhood.

I was distracted and hyperactive – today I probably would have been diagnosed as ADHD. I was always frustrated in school – unable to concentrate enough to study and do well on tests. My one sweet memory from elementary school was a teacher who did her best to make me feel like a child who mattered. When I didn't get any votes for class awards, she designated me "cutest student."

My stepfather took control of the family when he married my mother. Every two weeks, we were put on a bus to visit my father and stepmother in New York City. As I grew, my loneliness and isolation grew like a neglected weed. I was always angry, and most of the time I took out my anger on my siblings. The only time I felt a part of something good was when I visited the Dooley family up the street. They had six kids and their parents loved me like I was their own. I'd go there for sleepovers and tag along with them on family vacations. The kids and I would practice gymnastics and cheerleading, doing cartwheels on the grass and running along the sidewalks. It was the best part of my childhood – the rare occasions when the loneliness lifted for a while.

My life took a hard turn in the wrong direction at 11. My stepfather left, and I began to experience mood swings. It was later diagnosed as a symptom of bipolar disorder, but at the time I just felt angry – at my mother and at the entire world.

As I look back on that time, I realize how strong and brave my mother was. This had to be the most difficult period of her life. She had four kids by this time, and worked three jobs to support our family – without a car. But no matter what the circumstances, she never, *ever* complained. I can close my eyes and see her trudging up the street through the snow, hunched forward from the weight of the grocery bags she was carrying. Still, not a complaint. She never even mentioned the hardship she woke up to every day.

That summer, my life took a horrific turn that would haunt and scar me forever. I was sent to stay with family friends in Florida. A couple who lived nearby had two children I played with regularly. I'd sometimes spend the night there, but these sleepovers became real-life nightmares.

The first time I was invited to sleep there I was really excited, but my happiness turned to fear in the middle of the night. Imagine being just 11 years old and being awakened in the dark by a monster in the room. The monster touched me in places I knew no one should touch me. It happened again and again that summer. I would close my eyes and pray that the monster wouldn't come back, but he always did. I pretended to be asleep, but it didn't stop him. I dreaded the moments he touched me, but felt powerless to stop him. I knew he was wrong, but I was scared and ashamed. I guarded my dirty secret for years, never telling a soul what the father in that house was doing to me.

What was wrong with me?

I didn't know enough about sex at that age to really understand what was happening to me. I only knew that sex was supposed to be something that happened when I was much older, and with a person I loved. What he did to me made me want to vomit.

Why would a grown man want to do this to a young girl?

The monster continued to molest me for two months, and I continued to keep it a secret. Like most young sexual abuse victims, I was afraid to tell anyone or ask for help. I felt dirty and ashamed, as If *I* was the one who had done something wrong. When I grew a little older, I felt guilty for not telling anyone. He could have been molesting other children. I never confessed my horrible secret to anyone until I was an adult, when I told my parents and Danny about it. But the damage was already done by then, and the guilt and shame had eaten away at my self-esteem for years.

After returning home from "summer vacation" in Florida, I became overwhelmed by my emotions. I had built up so much anger and fear inside, and I released it by lashing out at the world. I couldn't tell anyone my awful secret, but I could act out, and that's just what I did when I entered middle school.

I spun out of control. Middle school was not a time of learning for me. I drank and smoked pot. It didn't take long before I was moving to heavier drugs.

Schoolwork, which had always been difficult, now seemed impossible. I would watch my friends succeed in school and become frustrated and angry.

Why should I even try? I'm flunking anyway.

I believed I wasn't capable of achieving in the academic arena, so I rarely put forth the effort to keep up with my classes.

When I entered high school, I found a friend. Julie Fisher and I became inseparable. I still struggled academically and emotionally, but having her in my life made it bearable. Julie always had a boyfriend, but I could never open up enough to have one myself. I never felt worthy, or pretty, or popular, like my brother and sister. I always felt like there was something wrong with me. But then I found a guy who paid attention to me, and a new nightmare began.

I was 16, and entered into a relationship with a 22-year-old man. The loneliness lifted again, at least for a while. I was thrilled that a popular guy like him would even notice me, never mind like me. I moved in with him when I was 17. It was such a relief having someone else to lean on – someone who seemed to want me around. So at the tender age of 19, I married him.

CHAPTER 2

*"Man may have discovered fire, but women
discovered how to play with it."*

- *Candace Bushnell, Sex and the City* -

Most people consider marriage to be something you should enter into when you are finished with school, settled down, and in love. For me, marriage was an escape from loneliness. Instead of following the traditional steps one takes to reach goals in life, I threw away those opportunities. I dropped out of high school to get married. My girlfriend Julie convinced me that enrolling in community college would be a smart move, so I followed her advice and registered for classes. Then my new husband and I launched into a full "college partying" experience. Our lives were a continuous celebration of smoking pot and drinking alcohol.

I soon discovered that I was pregnant. Despite the fact that I had little stability in my life, I couldn't help but be happy about this news. I wanted a baby – a baby girl. I wanted a baby girl so badly that even when the doctor told me the heart rate indicated it was a boy, I insisted that people only bring pink gifts to my baby shower. I was certain I would have a girl, and I would name her Jessica.

My husband had something growing in him, too – an addiction to more hardcore drugs, like cocaine. In my heart, I knew I needed to create a different kind of life for my baby, but instead of preparing for parenthood my husband was turning into a monster before my eyes. The beatings began.

The first time was a day I came home from work unexpectedly with a horrible case of morning sickness. All I wanted to do was sleep. But when I walked into the apartment, a full-blown party was going on. I screamed my indignation and insisted that everyone leave. My husband was furious. As soon as the last person cleared out, he pulled me by my hair and threw me to the floor. He began punching, hitting, and kicking me. Terrified, all I could do was try to protect my pregnant belly. When it was over, I was covered in bruises from head to toe. From then on, every complaint from me was answered with a beating from him. I know I sound like a foolish stereotype, but like many women who become abuse victims, I didn't leave. I thought it would stop once my baby arrived.

The day Jessica was born was one of the happiest days of my life. I had a natural delivery, with a midwife assisting me. I gave birth to a baby girl, just as I knew I would. She was healthy, and I was determined to keep her protected and content. Breastfeeding gave me a sense of security – I felt like I was doing something important to keep my baby healthy. I was amazed by the depth of my love for my little girl. I had experienced a lifetime of loneliness, but when Jessica came into my world the loneliness disappeared. She filled a void in which I had lived for my entire life.

My husband never hurt Jessica, but he continued to use me as his punching bag. By the time she was six months old, I knew I had to get out. I was desperately in need of money, so I found a job. One night while I was working and my husband was home with the baby, I felt a powerful mother's instinct and knew that I had to get home to my baby as soon as possible. I left work and arrived home to discover my husband and his friends using cocaine. A mattress had been set up to block the entrance to the kitchen, and Jessica was in her crib, screaming. Her diaper was falling off, and her face was so red I knew she had been crying frantically for hours. I calmed Jessica, bathed her, and called my mother. She made me promise I would leave, and I agreed to do it.

Late that night, after his friends left, my husband came into the bedroom where I was asleep. He woke me up and gave me the worst beating ever. He was so strong, and each blow was harder and more painful than the one before it. I fought back as hard as I could, but I was no match for him. He finally stopped, and I thought:

Is this love?
> *Why am I here?*
>> *What's wrong with me?*

The next day while my husband was at work, I kept my promise to my mother. I packed up Jessica and a few belongings and escaped. I had to leave and never look back. I couldn't bear to revisit the reasons I felt I deserved to be beaten and thought it was okay for a husband to treat his wife so horribly. I never wanted to put Jessica in harm's way, and I knew it was my responsibility to protect her – to protect both of us.

I divorced him and took classes to become a bartender. The bartending helped me earn a good living and I was soon able to afford an apartment. My family was a huge help to me – my mother was always willing to take care of Jessica. My sister, who also had a baby, shared the apartment with me.

I was very vigilant and protective of Jessica, and eventually, my husband accepted that our relationship was over. He left both Jessica and me alone. I continued to raise Jessica while working as a bartender, waitress, and legal secretary. Being a single mother was tough, and it was often hard to keep going. I had no idea that better times were ahead, and that one of the most wonderful gifts of my life was about to be revealed.

CHAPTER 3

"We plan our lives according to a dream that came to us
in childhood, and we find that life alters our plans.
And yet, at the end, from a rare height,
We also see that our dream was our fate.
It's just that providence had other ideas
As to how we would get there.
Destiny plans a different route, or turns the dream around,
as if it were a riddle, and fulfills the dream
In ways we couldn't have expected."

- Ben Okri -

I t was February 2, 1987, and I was about to experience a miracle. I was at a club called Jazzberries when Danny Trant walked into my life. The first time I saw him I remember thinking to myself, "That is the most gorgeous man I have ever seen." Danny was six foot, two inches tall, with short brown hair and gorgeous green eyes.

It wasn't until later that night that he noticed me too. I was wearing a beautiful yellow dress, cut low in the back. Danny turned to his friend and said, "I'm going to marry that girl." Of course, nobody imagined it would really come to pass.

Several weeks later, I was at work – I also had a job as a legal secretary – and my boss told me that there was a guy who worked at the District Attorney's office that had a crush on me. He said the guy wanted to take me out on a date. I was a little hesitant, but of course I was flattered. And curious. I told my boss I'd consider it if he would first point the guy out to me.

At the time, Danny worked at the District Attorney's office as a Victim Witness Advocate. Apparently, he had seen me come in and out of the office, but I wasn't aware of it.

When my boss showed me who it was, I couldn't believe my eyes. It was the guy I had seen at Jazzberries! Danny Trant. There was no doubt in my mind – I was definitely going to accept his offer for a date.

Our first date was unforgettable. The moment we looked into each other's eyes, we knew we could never spend another moment apart. He had invited me to join him at a friend's apartment because the friend was away. We had Chinese food to eat, an apartment to ourselves, and plenty of time to talk.

Conversation came so easily with Danny. I talked about my daughter, Jessica. He told me about his career as a professional basketball player, his happy childhood, and many other stories. I was riveted as he spoke. Just looking at him and listening to him talk gave me butterflies in my stomach.

Later that evening, he was playing in a basketball game. I went with him to watch the game, and I couldn't believe how talented he was. Danny was an amazing basketball player. After the game, we continued to talk . . . all night long. During the weeks that followed, I learned more about Danny, and everything I learned filled me with love and admiration.

Danny had grown up in Westfield, Massachusetts, the seventh of nine children. He never spoke an unloving word about his family, so I knew they were responsible for the incredibly kind and charismatic man he had become.

As a child, sports were everything to him. He practiced his favorite – basketball – for hours on end. Even during the winter, Danny would shovel the snow in the school parking lot across the street just to practice. He told me that the first basket he ever scored had gone into the opponent's net during his first basketball game, but it didn't discourage him. Danny was incredibly disciplined and persistent, and setbacks – no matter how major or minor – didn't stop him from succeeding at the game he loved.

In high school, he'd had a growth spurt that put him at his full height of 6 foot 2 inches. It was during his high school years that Danny developed into an outstanding athlete in both basketball and soccer. He once scored six soccer goals in a single game.

Danny continued to play in soccer and basketball leagues as he entered adulthood. At Clark University he was an athletic superstar – playing soccer and Division III basketball. When he graduated in 1984, he was drafted by the Boston Celtics, and continued to play professional basketball in Ireland. After two years, he returned to the United States to play for the Springfield Fame in the U.S. Basketball League, helping his team win the championship. During his basketball career, Danny was twice named an All American Basketball Player.

It's true that Danny had many amazing accomplishments to his credit, but that wasn't what attracted me to him. It was his heart—he had a heart of gold. From the beginning, I knew Danny was the man I had been waiting for all my life. All the hardship, all the loneliness, all the abuse and pain and tears faded into the past, and I felt like I was entering a beautiful and loving place with Danny. It was all so new and wonderful to me. I couldn't believe it was happening to me, but once I accepted my good fortune I believed it would stretch on forever.

CHAPTER 4

"Don't marry the person you think you can live with; marry only the individual you think you can't live without."

- James C. Dobson -

I remember the day I was certain Danny Trant was my soul mate – March 17th, St. Patrick's Day. I was supposed to bartend that night, but fortunately, I had found someone to cover for me. I wanted to surprise Danny and spend the evening with him. Seeing the excitement on his face when I showed up to see him set my heart fluttering the way it always did when I was around him. The feeling was so intense, I have to believe it was my subconscious telling me that I had found the person I had been searching for all of my life. At that moment, I just knew that we would spend the rest of our lives together.

But believe me, I was still boggled by the idea that a man like Danny would love a woman like me. I know no one is perfect, but I was (and remain) eccentric and quirky – not the kind of girl an average guy falls in love with. Plus, I had overwhelming feelings of insecurity, and my self-esteem was nonexistent.

Every day that Danny continued to stay by my side, I would ask myself:

What does this man see in me?

I never considered myself attractive, but Danny thought I was beautiful. Early in our relationship, we ran into one of his old girlfriends, and trust me, she was gorgeous. Strangely, I wasn't intimidated by this. Danny made me feel completely secure – he let me know that he was with me because he *wanted* to be with me and nobody else. He chose me, not her. I have never felt more beautiful – on the inside and the outside – than I did when I was with Danny. There was never a doubt in my mind about his love for me.

Three months after we started dating, Danny and I decided to get married. Just like that. We found a Justice of the Peace and invited a few people to join us. Our wedding was very casual, but we had so much fun. We couldn't afford a real reception or gathering, but our guests didn't care. They were happy to share this moment with us.

The most memorable moment of the wedding was when Danny introduced one of his friends to me and he exclaimed to Danny, "That's the girl in the backless yellow dress we saw at Jazzberries! You know, the girl you said you were going to marry!"

He was right!

After the wedding, we all went back to our home to relax and enjoy the occasion. I wore sweatpants while we ate cake to celebrate the beginning of the rest of our lives. In keeping with "wedding reception" tradition, Danny squashed a piece of cake in my face. Laughter and joy filled our home. I was happy. Really happy.

My family was delighted that Danny and I had gotten married. "He is a mother-in-law's dream come true!" my mother would say. My brothers and sisters were crazy about him. My daughter, Jessica, had already developed a strong bond with Danny, and he immediately became a beloved father figure to her. He intuitively set boundaries that made her feel secure. When a friend invited us to go on a boat trip as a honeymoon, he insisted on taking Jessica along, even though my mother offered to watch her.

As Danny and I began our lives as a married couple, I felt like I was living a fairy tale. After all the years of fear, sorrow, and loneliness, I had finally found my true love. Nobody had ever loved me the way Danny did. I felt like the luckiest woman on the planet to have him as my husband and as a father figure to my daughter.

From the beginning, Danny loved Jessica. We would later have two sons together, but there was never a bit of difference between the love he showed for his sons and the love he showed Jessica.

Jessica's biological father had minimal contact with her and never paid child support, but I still maintained a strong relationship with his parents. I wanted Jessica to know her grandparents. I did not want her to go through what I went through as a child of divorce – shuttling back and forth between homes.

Danny treated Jessica as if she was his own daughter, and he wanted to make it official. He asked to legally adopt Jessica. Showing true determination and courage, he went to Jessica's biological father himself.

He told him, "You have three choices. You can go to jail because you haven't paid the $50,000 in back child support that you owe my wife. You can pay it now. The third choice—and this is the one that I would love for you to take – is to let me adopt Jessica. I promise you that I will give her the best life she could possibly have." He chose the best option for everyone.

On March 2, 1989, Danny formally adopted Jessica and announced that she was his daughter. My parents and Danny's parents were so happy.

Danny and I both cried tears of joy. We all went out for a celebratory dinner. Life was so, so good.

Years later, a friend of Danny's told Jessica, "Your father once told me that the happiest day of his life was the day that he adopted you."

CHAPTER 5

"Family means putting your arms around each other and being there."

- Barbara Bush -

Before Danny met me, he had been planning to resume his professional basketball career in Ireland. But he wanted to remain close to Jessica and me, so he kept his job at the District Attorney's office. Over the next few years, we grew as a family, experiencing many days of joy. But like all families, we faced many challenges, too.

Just three months after we married, our family was faced with our first crisis. I collapsed because of an ectopic pregnancy that nearly turned fatal. This close encounter with death was very frightening for our entire family, and it took a while to recover. A year and a half later, we had a second miscarriage. Danny and I were devastated.

Would Jessica be our only child?

I was discouraged, but in my heart I never doubted that eventually we would have more children.

This period of our life was what I called our "hungry years" because sometimes, after paying the bills, we only had about $20 left to buy groceries. Of course, we never went hungry, but Danny and I both had to work very hard to support the family. Danny was in charge of the finances, and he always made sure the bills were paid. Even though money was always tight, we didn't allow financial concerns to cast a shadow over our family. We were a team, and we worked together well.

Jessica never knew of our money troubles, and we wanted it that way. We were still able to give her vacations, because I had relatives who lived in the Hamptons. We'd visit there periodically, loving every minute we could spend on the beach. The beaches of the New York Hamptons are among the most beautiful in the world. Jessica, Danny, and I loved to stay late and watch the sun set over the ocean. I remember these trips as some of the best times of our lives.

As time passed, I struggled with mood swings, which was actually my undiagnosed bipolar disorder. I was able to manage much of this without medication, simply because Danny made me feel so joyful. He was so easygoing and understanding. He accepted me for who I was, mood swings and all. When I was feeling anxious about something, he would reassure me. "If there is nothing you can do about it, then just don't worry about it." It was simple to him, and he made it easier for me.

At last, we become pregnant again. We were both thrilled. Jessica was only six years old and I knew that she was curious about where the baby came from. I wanted to be truthful with her about it, so I went to the library and checked out an age-appropriate video about how life begins. Jessica and I watched it together and talked about it.

I became hugely pregnant. The baby was enormous! We brought Jessica with us to an ultrasound appointment, and we were all overjoyed when we found out it was a boy. Danny and I both had been praying for a boy because Danny wanted Jessica to feel like she was special – his only little girl. When the technician told us the baby was, in fact, a boy, Jessica and Danny held each other and jumped up and down. Just like when he had adopted Jessica, Danny and I cried tears of joy.

Our baby boy was born on March 22, 1989, delivered with the help of a midwife. I had no pain medication, despite the baby's size – he was nearly 11 pounds and 24 inches long! Danny was so proud of me. We decided I would breastfeed the baby because we wanted him to be as healthy as possible.

A few months after our son was born, I had another miscarriage, but that sadness was soon replaced with another miracle. This time around, we decided let the baby's gender be a surprise. Deep down, I knew it was a boy and I prayed that God would give us another little boy to love. But the rest of the family was convinced that I would have another girl.

It was a boy!

After our second son was born, we decided that I wouldn't return to work. I stayed home and cared for the children while Danny worked extremely hard to support our family. He continued on at the District Attorney's office, and found a second job loading trucks for Consolidated Freight. Danny was an excellent provider, and always tried to find ways to increase our income so I could stay home.

CHAPTER 6

"The family. We were a strange little band of characters trudging through life sharing disease and toothpaste, coveting one another's desserts, hiding shampoo, borrowing money, locking each other out of our rooms, inflicting pain and kissing to heal it in the same instant, loving, laughing, defending, and trying to figure out the common thread that bound us all together."

- Erma Bombeck -

D anny was such a kind and generous man. Good looking, too. He wore nice clothes for work, but dressed like an athlete when he was home. Sneakers were definitely his favorite item when it came to spending money – he had a real weakness for new sneakers. But no matter what he needed, he would always buy something for the children or me before he would spend money on himself. He was not the least bit selfish.

They say that good things come to those who wait, and that proved to be true for our family. In 1991, Danny received a referral for a possible bond trader position through a connection he had made during his career as a professional athlete. The position was in New York City. He was scheduled for a job interview, and interestingly enough, the person interviewing him – his potential boss – was going to take him to a basketball game.

Soon after the interview was scheduled, my sister called to tell me she had two tickets to the Grammy Awards and she wanted me to go with her. But since Danny's interview would overlap the show, I needed to stay home with the children. I told Danny about the invitation and reminded him that it was a chance of a lifetime. I had expected him to help me find someone to stay with the kids, but instead he called to cancel the interview.

Danny told his potential boss, "Unfortunately, I can't go to the basketball game with you. My wife has a chance to go to the Grammy Awards with her sister, so I need to stay with my kids."

You might expect that this would kill any chances Danny had of getting hired, but the interviewer completely understood. Without a moment's hesitation, he replied, "We need family men like you! You're hired!"

Danny went to New York to start his new job and find us a place to live, while the children and I stayed with my mother. I was so excited about moving to our new home in New York, and I was thrilled about Danny's new career opportunity. But it's never easy to make a new home with three children in an unfamiliar city.

When we first moved to New York, I felt very isolated. I worried about how the move would affect Jessica, since she had already moved several times in her short life. Also, our finances would continue to be a source of stress until Danny could work his way up the career ladder. But we confronted all of these challenges together, and we were able to overcome the obstacles we faced as a team.

As our children grew, we settled into a very comfortable family routine. I loved every minute of life as Danny's wife and as mother to my children. On weekdays, Danny would wake up at 4:30 a.m. to commute to work while I got the children off to school. Then I'd clean the house, do laundry, and cook dinner. I always tried to take an active role in my children's education by volunteering at their school, so I did a lot of that. When Danny was home in the evenings, he would take the children to a sporting event. When they returned we would have some private time together, even if it was just watching television in bed.

Danny's new position as a bond trader was very demanding, but he loved his job. He was so intelligent it didn't take him long to learn the trade – it came naturally to him. Danny would compare the excitement of bond trading to the rush of participating in a competitive sport. His work schedule was exhausting, but he never complained. He laughed when he told me about falling asleep while leaning against a pole on the train during his morning commute. It took years, but eventually he worked his way up the corporate ladder, increasing his salary as he progressed. He was great at his position because he was naturally a people person. Everyone loved working with him – a hard worker who was also fun to be around.

Danny and I were inseparable, even when it came to work events. Occasionally, he would have to entertain clients, and he enjoyed bringing me along even though his colleagues typically didn't include their wives. He liked having me by his side. We always made it a point, though, to give each other time to ourselves and time to spend with other people. We were both trusting, and we encouraged each other to maintain our friendships. He enjoyed time with his guy friends as much as I enjoyed my girlfriends.

I loved being a stay-at-home mom, and I believe it was something I did really well. Since I volunteered so frequently at the children's' school, I became the class mom. It meant a lot to me to spend time with my children, not only to ensure that they received an excellent education, but to nurture their distinct personalities. Each of the children was so special to me, and I loved being able to witness their growing-up years so closely.

Jessica was an active, feisty little girl from the day she was born. At eight months, she was not only walking, but climbing stairs and getting into everything. From the moment she learned how to talk, she was outspoken. She would speak her mind about everything, and she could be incredibly comical. Even today, Jessica remains very straightforward about letting people know what she thinks. It's a trait she and I share, and unfortunately, it can get us into trouble.

I always suspected that Jessica and I also shared the tendency toward ADHD, but from an early age, Jess found a way to channel it into something positive and productive. Sports. Jessica was a natural athlete who was unafraid to try out for different sports - basketball, track, swimming, dance, and soccer – she tried them all. But it was soccer that gave her an opportunity to really shine. It also gave her many opportunities to travel throughout the U.S. and Canada. One summer, Jessica was one of 15 girls who were chosen to be on a select soccer team. Both Danny and I were so proud of her because hundreds of girls had tried out.

My older son was the most sociable of the three children. Jessica and my younger son were typically homebodies while my older son loved being out all the time with his friends. He was also an unusually kind child – not an ounce of meanness in him. He was so gentle and kind to everyone he came in contact with, including his siblings.

One memory of his childhood stays with me as if it happened yesterday. When he was in second grade, his class put on a play where the parents were responsible for making their own child's costume. After I had finished making his bird costume for him, I noticed he was trying to make another bird costume. I thought maybe he didn't approve of the one I had made, so I asked him about it. His response made me so proud to be his mother. "Mommy," he said, "There's a boy in my class who said his mother won't make him a costume. So I'm going to make him one myself!" He also insisted that I pick up the little boy and take him to the play, because his own mother couldn't.

As a teenager, my older son became even more like his father – an excellent athlete. He was also very interested in learning about religion, especially Catholicism. Danny and I agreed that we should allow our children to make up their own minds about religion. They needed to choose their own spiritual paths. Our elder son chose to attend a Catholic high school for two years before attending a local public high school. When he later became interested in exploring Buddhism, we didn't discourage him.

My younger son is one of the most intelligent human beings I have ever known. He always had an uncanny memory for detail. At five years old, he was riding in the back seat of the car with Jessica and her friend. In the course of 15 minutes, they taught him how to do multiplication and division. There was never any reason to argue with him about anything, because he would always win. Even as a very young child he could find a way to convince you that he was right.

Like Jessica, he was very humorous child. When he was about two years old, he was playing with some toys, and muttered aloud, "Stupid!"

Overhearing him, my husband asked, "What did you say?"

"Stupid," my son repeated, as if there was nothing wrong with the word.

Danny explained, "That's not a nice word to say."

"Okay, stupid," my son replied under his breath as he walked away. Even though his father's lecture had misfired, we couldn't help but laugh at his response.

CHAPTER 7

*"It takes tremendous discipline to control the influence,
the power you have over other people's lives."*

- Clint Eastwood -

D anny was such a wonderful husband and father, and nobody had to remind me of this. But other women often told me they wished their husbands were more like Danny. The first time my friend Susie met Danny, I wasn't there, but she told me about it. Susie was at a basketball game Danny was playing in and my sons were sitting in the stands, watching their father play. Our younger son was still in diapers, and at some point during the game, he needed a diaper change. Danny stopped the whole game, calmly changed the diaper, and then went back to playing the game. When she told me about it later, she said, "At that moment, I fell in love with your husband."

Not only was Danny a terrific partner and parent, he was an inspiring coach. Literally hundreds of children received guidance – athletic and otherwise – from Danny over the years. He coached athletically gifted children who played on Amateur Athletic Union (AAU) basketball teams, but he also devoted his time to coaching children who were not as accomplished. He would tell them, "You're not going to be professional basketball players, but because you are here, making an effort, you're going to be good at something." This affirmation was such a gift to the children.

When Danny coached AAU basketball, our family grew close to an eleven year old boy named Terrell, who played on our older son's team. Terrell worshipped Danny, and it didn't take all of us long to feel the same way about Terrell. Both of Terrell's parents worked two jobs, so his grandmother cared for him much of the time. Terrell soon began staying with our family almost every weekend. Eventually, he became our godson. We loved him like our own child, and he went everywhere with us. Terrell had a loving family of his own, and we grew to consider all of them a part of our family.

Before Terrell came into our lives, he was struggling in school, but his relationship with Danny helped him focus and succeed. He became an athletic superstar and graduated from Xavier College. When I attended one of his college basketball games, he called me down from the stands and gave me a big hug in front of the entire stadium. Then, he walked onto the basketball court and played the game on behalf of Danny. It took my breath away.

Terrell has remained close to our family, and I know that Danny would be so proud of his achievements.

Terrell is an example of the amazing way Danny was able to reach out and connect with children of all ages. He was a very self-disciplined person, so he understood the importance of discipline for children.

As soon as Danny met Jessica, he set boundaries for her because she was so much like me—she had a mind of her own and could be difficult. For Danny, there were no gray areas, and Jessica quickly learned that she couldn't wiggle her way out of doing what was right.

When Danny disciplined his own children or the children he coached, he didn't raise his voice or make derogatory comments. Instead, he used his quiet voice with a tone of authority that children never questioned. They would look up at him, their big eyes taking in everything he said, and immediately adjusted their behavior. He often tried to incorporate humor while motivating the children to behave.

When the boys misbehaved, I didn't feel confident about disciplining them myself, so if Danny wasn't home, I would call him and put him on speakerphone. All he had to say was, "All right, ladies," he'd tease, "what are you doing now?" Without an argument, they would respond, "Sorry, Dad." That would be the end of it—problem solved.

It was fortunate for me that Danny was great at effectively disciplining the children, because I had never been any good at it. My painful childhood memories made it extremely difficult for me to come down on my children at all, even when they needed discipline. I just wanted them to be happy and not worry about any parental disapproval.

Even though I usually depended on Danny to handle discipline, we always talked about the issue and came to a resolution together. Once, when Danny withheld our son's privileges for a week as a result of a small incident, I told him I thought a week was too long for the offense committed. Danny and I came to an agreement that a lighter punishment was more appropriate. These parenting discussions were never conducted in front of the children. A wise person once told me, "If you disagree with your husband about how to handle the kids, don't ever argue about it in front of them. Instead, go into the bedroom, close the door, and talk about it calmly and privately." I always tried to follow that advice.

I never wanted to deprive my children of anything. They had quite a bit more in the way of material things than I did growing up, but I don't think they were ever spoiled. All three of them were very grateful for and generous with the money we gave them, and they were delighted to treat their friends.

As a mother, I tended to be overprotective. I constantly worried about my children's safety. I wouldn't even allow my sons to ride a bicycle until they were thirteen years old because I always imagined something awful happening to them when they were out of my sight. Probably because of the molestation I had endured as a child, I was tormented by fear that my children might be vulnerable to sexual abuse. To help protect them, I educated them in age-appropriate ways about sex. I explained to them that their bodies were beautiful, but they belonged only to themselves, and they should never allow anyone else to touch their bodies without permission.

CHAPTER 8

"One of the things that binds us as a family is a shared sense of humor."

- Ralph Fiennes -

I have so many happy memories of our life together as a family. There was always so much laughter in our home. Danny could bring us all to hysterics over just about anything. He didn't need a lot of material – anything in everyday life was jokeworthy in the Trant house.

Danny loved to sing as he walked around the house. If anybody else had done this, it would have annoyed me to no end, but Danny had a great voice. As a child, he accompanied his mother to nursing homes, where he'd sing for the residents. Danny knew the words and melodies to almost any television theme song – *Leave it to Beaver, I Dream of Jeannie, the Courtship of Eddie's Father* – and we'd make a game out of it. We would mention a TV show and within seconds he would be singing the show's theme song. He loved soul music, especially songs by the Stylistics. At karaoke bars, he'd sing *My Love* to me. Once, as he was singing karaoke, a woman yelled out, "I want to marry you!" Danny didn't miss a beat. He pointed to me and responded, "I'm already married!"

Birthdays and holidays were a very big deal in our house. For our twenty-fifth birthdays, we gave each other a surprise birthday party, inviting a huge crowd of our family and friends. At each birthday celebration, we could count on a few laughs over my grandmother's gifts – they were always a variation on hideous clothing she found at the Salvation Army store. Thrifty, but definitely not stylish. Still, we loved them because they came from someone who was special to us.

Thanksgiving was one of our favorite holidays. The day before Thanksgiving, Danny and I would have a gathering with a group of friends from our past. For Easter, we loved to take the children to Florida to visit Danny's family and go to Disney World.

Life wasn't always perfect, though it came pretty close. But like all married couples, Danny and I had issues that came up, and we made sure we didn't brush them off – we were determined to deal with them. We even went to therapy together to resolve some of our roadblocks. Our biggest issue revolved around my insecurities and brokenness compared with Danny's self-confidence and security. This huge difference often made me feel like I was a burden to him, but he didn't see it that way. He was aware of all of my flaws before we were married, but loved me despite them. Danny understood I was hyper-sensitive and easily upset by many things, but he didn't see it as a negative. He would just tell me my heart was too big.

Instead of criticizing me when my personality got me into trouble, he would try to find ways to help me change my behavior. For example, when Jessica began playing soccer, I became an obnoxious soccer mom. At the games, I would often yell out off-color comments. Later, Danny would call me out on it, and I'd go overboard with self-loathing. When that happened, he'd remind me, "Everyone makes mistakes. It's not the end of the world."

I moved on and learned the right way to conduct myself when I was cheering my children on at sporting events. When I became a basketball mom, I had learned to keep my obnoxious comments to myself. Danny helped me learn to just sit back and enjoy watching my children play.

Early in our marriage, Danny and I had some heated arguments, but as time went on, everything somehow clicked. By the time we entered our thirties, we rarely argued. If we did become angry with one another, we would just go to separate rooms to wait for the tension to dissipate, and then come together again. Our love life was unbelievable. Intimacy was an important part of our marriage and we never lost the romantic connection.

Danny respected that I had a mind of my own, but also appreciated my "kooky" side. During the 2000 Presidential Election, the "hanging chads" controversy made me livid. I was so upset about it that my husband challenged me to go to Washington, D.C. and do something about it. My friend and I thought that was a great idea, so we traveled to Washington, D.C. to protest outside the Supreme Court. We were thrilled that we'd be part of a demonstration of thousands of concerned Americans just like ourselves. We made posters that said "All we are saying is, let the votes count." Unfortunately, there were only three of us out there standing up for our beliefs in the frigid weather. No sign of the thousands of protestors we had expected.

My husband usually voted for whatever Democratic candidate was running, but during the New York State Senate election, he was considering voting for the Republican candidate. I love Hillary Clinton, so I threatened, "Don't you dare cancel out my vote for Hillary. If you do, you're sleeping on the couch!" He laughed and responded, "Okay, but I'm bringing the boys with me into the voting booth. I'll let them pull the lever for Hillary so I don't have to." When he returned from voting, the boys announced, "We voted for the right person!"

Even though Danny joked about politics, he was always a person of principle. He did not tolerate prejudice or discrimination of any kind. Danny was raised as a Catholic, and he insisted on having our children baptized. But as an adult, he had strong objections to the way he felt the church discriminated against the lesbian, gay, bisexual, and transgender community. He was also quite upset that we were not able to marry in a Catholic Church.

We faced a major ordeal when the boys were quite young. Like all families, life is full of challenges, but this one really scared us. When my older son was 10, he was stricken with a mysterious eye disease. At first the doctor thought it was pink eye, but the prescribed medication didn't alleviate the symptoms. We took him to a specialist, who said our son had uveitis, an autoimmune disease that causes the body to attack the site of an infection. In this case, the white blood cells would attack the irises, causing scar tissue to form and eventually, blindness. Six months after receiving this devastating news, our younger son was diagnosed with the same thing. Doctors were convinced that both boys would be legally blind by the time they were 21.

This was a very difficult time for our family, but Danny and I knew we had to stay strong and work together to care for our children. We were determined to find the best course of action, so we traveled to hospitals around the country to consult with the nation's best doctors.

During one six-month period, Danny and I had to treat the boys' eyes with steroid drops every thirty minutes around the clock. Maintaining this treatment regimen was exhausting. We would sleep with a stopwatch marking off thirty-minute intervals, and take turns administering the medicine.

Years later, my son's jaw swelled and he began having trouble walking. It was then that we learned the source of the problem for both boys: Juvenile Rheumatoid Arthritis. The doctors said it was rare for siblings to have this disease, so we remained skeptical and kept searching for answers.

One day in August of 2001, not long before he died, Danny was in the furnace room in the basement of our house. He saw something growing on the walls that alarmed him. We had experts come in to determine exactly what it was, and learned that it was black mold. It was imperative that we get rid of the mold completely for health reasons, and that required gutting almost our entire house. Workers were in the process of completing this mold abatement when Danny died the next month.

Danny and I struggled quite a bit with Jessica as she grew older. She was quite beautiful and Danny was always afraid someone would take advantage of her, so he was very protective. He would joke about putting her in lockdown for several years to keep her safe. Jess rebelled against the restrictions put on her, and during her senior year of high school she ran away from home. We were devastated – neither of us knew where she was or what she was doing for a week. We were concerned for her safety and her future – we knew if she stopped going to school she would lose a soccer scholarship that had been offered to her at Pace University. We soon discovered that she was staying nearby at a friend's house.

Danny approached this crisis with his usual calm determination, but I was totally distraught. I lashed out at Danny, accusing him of not caring about where our daughter was. Later, I heard him sobbing in the shower. I knew this was something Danny felt deeply, because he was not one to cry easily. He told me that he loved Jessica with all his heart, and knew she would come back. Danny said that we needed to allow Jessica to learn how to do the right thing on her own. After about a week, Jessica did return home, just as Danny had predicted.

I remember him crying only two other times – when his nephew and his brother died within a short time period. Both deaths hit us very hard, but Danny was completely heartbroken. These tragedies were followed by another one when Jessica lost a close friend. The whole family was reeling and struggling to hold it together after these three wrenching losses. I held Danny in my arms as he wept for the people he loved so much.

By December of 2000, Danny and I had some financial breathing room, and were finally able to enjoy the gift life gave us next – our first house. I may not have been the first person ever to cry tears of joy during a home closing, but having a house to call our own was so incredibly special to us. Danny's work as a bond trader put us in a much better financial position, but we had been renting until we were sure we could handle a large mortgage. We wanted to take our time and spend our money on our children. We loved taking them on family vacations, and Danny insisted that we have the freedom to live life to the fullest.

A perfect marriage does not exist, and even Danny was not perfect. But in my mind, he came awfully close. Every day of his life, he tried to do the right thing. If he was wrong about something, he was the first to admit it. Some people were convinced that I didn't deserve Danny, and maybe they're right. But he *chose* to be with me because he loved me. We adored each other and there was nothing anyone could say to change that. In my heart, I know that I was a good wife to him, and I wanted nothing more than for him to be happy. Even after fourteen years of marriage, my heart fluttered when I saw him. That flutter never went away.

CHAPTER 9
Jessica's Perspective

"I know that I will never find my father in any other man who comes into my life because it is a void in my life that can only be filled by him."

- Halle Berry -

M y mother and I are like two peas in a pod. Both of us are unconventional and high-strung. At times, we can be hard to deal with. But my father, Daniel Trant, had a way of seeing us that turned our flaws into charming peculiarities that sparked his affection. The slightest setback would send my mother or me off the deep end, but my father took everything in stride.

My dad was an amazing guy – smart, good-looking, articulate, athletic, and witty – he had it all. He was incredibly charismatic, and his many positive features drew people to him. He had so many friends, and everyone seemed to love him as soon as they met him. He was extremely loyal and sentimental, and kept in contact with all of his friends from the past. When we visited his hometown it was as if the mayor was returning. Even though he hadn't lived there for many years, everyone knew him and was so happy to see him.

My mother and father were smitten with each other from the moment they met. My father adored my mother, and she worshipped him. He was never impulsive, so it must have been quite a shock to people that just three months after they started dating, he married a woman who already had a child from a previous marriage.

My parents were so close that it was as if they were a single person. Whatever one of them lacked, the other made up for. When they were apart, they talked on the phone constantly. As a child, I noticed how different they were from the other parents I knew. Friends were always mentioning how attractive my mother or father was, but it wasn't their good looks or physical displays of affection that made them special. It was the way they were always in sync with one another, which made it very pleasant to be around them.

I would never say that my parents had a perfect marriage, but their love never seemed to lose steam . . . it grew stronger and stronger as each year passed. They never settled for a dull marriage routine or the tense standoff that can happen in many long marriages. I remember hearing arguments when I was a small child, but after I entered high school, I heard nothing – no arguing or bickering at all. Our family did struggle with periods of stress, but that was kept from me. My parents didn't want me to have memories of discord, but only of family happiness and security.

My mother had a lot of insecurities, which my father never understood, because he adored her. He was convinced her poor self-image was rooted in her difficult childhood. Even though my mother was beautiful, she didn't see herself that way. She could never view herself in a positive light. Wherever she went, people would compliment her and men would flirt with her. Instead of being overcome with jealousy, my father would stand proud. Every day, my father would remind her of how beautiful she was. He hoped that this reassurance would help her move forward in a positive direction.

Everyone has flaws, and my father did too. He recognized my mother's flaws, but he loved her despite them. Sometimes she would act inappropriately and upset people, but my father always stood up for her. Unfortunately, both my mother and I have a hard time admitting we are wrong. We will fight to the death to prove that we're right, even when we are not. Sometimes my father would talk to her later, in private, about an incident that had occurred in public, but more often, he would allow her to vent.

I remember my father giving me a piece of advice: "I'm going to teach you a little lesson about your mother," he said. "Learn this lesson and you will go far in life. Just 'yes' her. Let her think she's right." He wasn't trying to be snide; he meant it. My father loved and understood her, and he accepted her completely. He may have tried to help her get along in the world a little better, but not once did he try to change who she was.

I never really knew my mother's first husband, who was my biological father. I have always had a relationship with his parents, who were my biological grandparents. I was only 6 months old when my mother left him because he abused drugs and physically abused her. I was never a part of his life plan, and he chose not to be involved in my life. My mother divorced him so that both of us could have better lives.

Before my father, Daniel Trant, adopted me, I was a bit of a holy terror because my mother had never disciplined me. The first time my father told me "no," I responded with a forceful, "Excuse me?" I quickly changed my attitude. His upbringing was strict, and he maintained firm standards of behavior for me and my brothers. I needed structure, and this firmer foundation worked well for me. I sometimes rebelled against it, but I'm glad I had it.

March 2, 1989 was the day my father adopted me. It remains one of the most important days of my life. It was always our special day. Every year on "our anniversary," he would take me out to dinner and a movie. He would give me flowers and a card that said "Happy Anniversary! Adopting you was the greatest thing I ever did." That was our tradition – just the two of us. Daughter and Dad.

Twenty days after the adoption was finalized, my first brother was born. I was only 6 years old. Before he was born, I remember my mother having me watch a video about the facts of life. She was always very open with me about sex, and sometimes my father would be so embarrassed that he would leave the room during the conversations.

Even though the prospect of expecting a baby brother was exciting, I felt like I had to compete with this intruder. It seemed like all of a sudden, the new baby was receiving all the attention, and that didn't sit well with me. Of course, he turned out to be a cute, sweet child, and I was thrilled. I am thankful it was a boy, though, because if it had been a girl, I might have made her life miserable!

A year later, my second brother was born, and this time my reaction was much different. Instead of becoming all bent out of shape, I decided I wanted this baby to be just like me. I was so obsessed with him that I would carry him around like he was my own baby. We were inseparable – just like my dad and my other brother were – joined at the hip.

Both of my brothers struggled with health issues at a young age, when they developed a serious eye condition. It started with my oldest brother and then my youngest brother was stricken with the same thing. At first, the doctors thought it was pink eye, but the antibiotics didn't help at all. Their eyes remained swollen. The doctors continued to run tests, pricking them constantly, but couldn't figure out what was causing the symptoms. They were puzzled by the fact my two siblings had the same symptoms, which led to theories like it being genetic or caused by a cat scratch.

Several years later, we discovered that black mold had been growing in our basement, where my brothers played when they were little. The mold had to be removed, which was a major undertaking, but everyone suspected that the mold might have triggered the boys' eye condition. They both went into remission, which was an incredible relief for everyone. But to this day we don't know what caused the eye disease.

As the enforcer of discipline, my father never once raised his hand or voice to my brothers or me. He just gave us "the look," which was discipline enough. Even adults would respond to that look, and do whatever he told them to do.

Like my mother, I automatically go into a defensive mode when I feel I am being attacked. I don't take criticism well. But somehow, even with "the look," my father never triggered that defensive reaction in me. When he provided constructive criticism, I didn't feel as if I was being attacked. His method was to offer me alternatives to how I could respond to a situation. He'd tell me to try doing something one way rather than the way I was doing it, just to see if it worked better. He never looked down on me, so I didn't feel like he was being condescending. The constructive criticism my father taught me is something I will use for the rest of my life.

In my teens, I was just like any other teenager – I rebelled. Being grounded was nothing out of the ordinary. My friends would always have to come to my house because I was usually grounded and couldn't go to their homes. I chafed a little at it, but later understood the importance of having discipline in my own life and in my relationships.

My dad was great at his job as a bond trader. One man told me something about my dad that I'll always remember. He said, "You already know what a great basketball player he was. But I'm going to tell you something else about him."

I thought I had heard it all, but I decided to hear him out. He continued, "I'm in the same industry as your father, and I invest millions of dollars. I make a really good living and I don't trust many people with my money, but I trusted your father. That means he was *really* good at his job."

I wasn't surprised by what the man said. My father always put in more effort than anyone else. But the amazing thing was that my dad wasn't even trained to be a bond trader! It just came naturally to him, like everything he did.

My dad was also great at being a good person, and I was always meeting people who told me how much they thought of him. Most of the stories people told me about him were focused on his basketball career or his sense of humor.

Sports were a huge thing in our family. My father would always say that I needed to either play a sport or get a job because a sport could help me pay for college. Ultimately, my interest in sports did pay off because I received a soccer scholarship to Pace University. My biological father's father was Italian, and he ran in the Olympics against Jesse Owens the year Hitler hosted the games. I believe I inherited my athleticism from that side of the family, but I got my fight from my mother and my strong will from my father, Danny. My mother has never been athletic, but she's a fierce competitor.

When it came to soccer, my parents were my biggest fans. My father motivated me to do my best. When I struggled to get out of bed for my morning run, he would offer to run with me. My father's nickname for me was "L.A.," which stood for "Lard Ass." It was a comical nickname because I obviously wasn't fat. During soccer games, he would call out, "Wheels, L.A., wheels!"

During my teens, my family struggled through a series of losses, including the death of my friend, who had cystic fibrosis. My father's nephew and brother died one after the other. My parents were always honest with my brothers and me. They never tried to hide the truth about the deaths or attempted to sugarcoat it. Without going into gory detail, they explained exactly what had happened, and encouraged us to express our feelings. They made sure we had a therapist or school guidance counselor available to provide additional support.

On top of caring for their children, my parents had to find a way to process their own grief. My mother's crying was nothing out of the ordinary for us, but it was extremely hard to hear my father cry. Before he met my mother, my father used to keep his emotions hidden. That's how he was raised. But my mother broke this barrier, enabling him to express his sadness. After that, he always looked to my mother for comfort. When his brother died, I heard my father wailing in the other room. My mother could be a little overboard emotionally, but at times like this she was able to help him. They balanced each other out.

Life changed quite a bit for me when I went away to college. I was on my own and, like any new college student; I made some mistakes. One night during my freshman year, I had to go to the hospital with alcohol poisoning. My soccer coach found out and told me I needed to tell my parents – or he would. Since I knew they were going to find out one way or another, I decided to just go ahead and get it over with.

When I called my father to tell him about it, all he said was, "Did you learn your lesson?" He told me to keep it from my mother. No reason to get her all upset over something that was in the past. I had learned my lesson.

When I returned home for the summer, my dad and I butted heads a bit about my curfew. He insisted I be home by midnight, which really upset me. When he said "If you don't like my rules, then don't live in my house," I overreacted. Instead of accepting his rules, I moved in with my college roommate, five houses down the street. I stayed with her the whole summer.

CHAPTER 10

"What we have done for ourselves alone dies with us; what we have done for others and the world remains and it is immortal."

- Albert Pike -

In the spring of 2001, I was taking a shower one day when I detected the scent of flowers. The scent was strongly reminiscent of funeral flowers, and I flashed on a visual of a memorial service. Somehow I knew that the memorial service was for Danny, though his body wasn't visible. I broke down in tears and immediately called Danny. My husband, of course, made a joke out of it. "It's because you give me food from McDonald's every night!" he joked. Even in moments of anguish, his teasing and laughter was reassuring, but that experience really rattled me.

A short time later, we were planning a surprise birthday celebration for Danny's 40th birthday, which was May 15th. I had decided to wait until June to throw the big surprise party for him, because I knew he wouldn't be expecting it in June. My friends and family helped me schedule the party for the day of our niece's graduation. Danny was under the impression that he was helping me prepare for the graduation celebration as he helped set up his own surprise party.

My sister offered to host the party at her house in the Hamptons. She had a beautiful home with a pool, and we invited more than 100 guests. At first, we had difficulty convincing Danny to come to the "graduation party," but I told him he had no choice – he couldn't let me go by myself. Finally, he agreed to go and said he would be bringing the boys and his godson along. I hadn't told the boys about the party, because they were never good at keeping secrets.

When Danny and the boys walked in the door, everyone shouted, "Surprise!" Danny was so touched that he started crying, so of course I started crying too. The memory of that party is etched in my mind forever. The weather was perfect. Friends and family surrounded us, inside and outside of the house. Steam rose from the heated pool, tables were overflowing with great food, and Danny's favorite champagne filled every glass.

Summer passed, and fall was just beginning. The first weekend of September, we went to the beach and stayed at a friend's cabana. We brought the boys, including Terrell, and had the most wonderful time. I had been injured in a car accident the week prior to this and I had to take it easy, but I was able to enjoy this time with my family. I remember Danny taking me down to the beach to walk, and as he held my hand, he told me how beautiful I was.

The following weekend, we visited my sister in the Hamptons. She had lost a dear friend and was quite upset, so she appreciated our support. Danny and my sister were always very close. When she started talking about her friend who had passed away, Danny gathered us both in his arms. I was sitting on one knee and my sister on the other. My sister wept. "This man was just like you," she said. "He was a man's man, and everyone loved him, but now he is gone."

Danny, the boys, and his best friend, Lance, were huge Red Sox fans. Lance had bought four tickets for the Red Sox and Yankees game scheduled for Monday, September 10th. They went to the stadium and hung around for a while, but the game was rained out. Lance drove back home with Danny and the boys, and Danny mentioned that he was planning to bring Lance and the boys with him to the office the next day.

The next day was Tuesday, September 11. When our alarm clock went off that morning, Danny and I lay together in bed for a while. We just looked into each other's eyes and talked about how much our older son had enjoyed himself at the rained-out game the night before, even though they didn't actually end up playing. Danny was pleased with the way they had all bonded.

While we chatted in our bedroom, the boys were getting ready to go to the office with their dad and Lance. I was uncomfortable with the idea of them missing school, and pointed out that a new school year was just beginning and our sons had missed thirty days of school the previous year because of their eye condition. Danny and I agreed that it was best for them not go to the office so they wouldn't fall further behind in school. Lance decided to stay behind, too. It terrifies me to imagine what might have happened if my children had accompanied Danny to work that day.

It was an absolutely beautiful day, with sunshine and blue skies. It was bright, and light, and I felt so happy and contented with my life on that beautiful Tuesday. I never could have imagined what a dark place that day would lead to, for years to come. As Danny walked out the door, he kissed me and I waved goodbye. It would be the last time I ever saw him. My soul mate and the love of my life. My everything – *gone.*

CHAPTER 11

"September 11ᵗʰ was a reminder that life is fleeting, impermanent, and uncertain. Therefore, we must make use of every moment and nurture it with affection, tenderness, beauty, creativity, and laughter."

- Deepak Chopra, M.D. -

It was such a perfect day, I wanted to get the full fresh-air experience. So I decided to walk to Dunkin' Donuts to buy coffee and a bagel. When I walked back into the house, the phone was ringing. I answered it, and heard Danny's voice. I immediately knew something was wrong. There was an urgency in his voice when he said, "Kathy, do you have the television on?" When I told him no, he responded, "Just listen to me."

"What?" I asked, "What do you mean?"

He said firmly, "Kathy, for once, you cannot talk. You have to listen to me."

I agreed, as my heart pounded in my chest and my legs felt like they could barely hold me upright.

"A plane has crashed into our building, Kathy. There is smoke everywhere. I can hardly breathe. I don't know how long I'll be able to stay on the phone with you." He barely paused and said, "I want you to know that I love you and the kids more than life itself, and you have to promise me you'll be strong."

I cried, "What are you talking about?" I screamed for Lance to turn on the television. On the screen I saw the smoke coming out of the World Trade Center tower where Danny's office was located. I understood then that my husband was trapped inside. I immediately began to go into shock.

Danny continued, "I love you, Kathy. I'll see you on the other side. I promise I'll see you again."

The phone went dead.

I was too scared to get hysterical. I couldn't even feel my body – only my heart pounding with fear. As we watched a second plane crash into the other tower, I nearly collapsed as I was overcome with fear and helplessness. I just wanted Danny to call back and tell me he'd made it out okay. I prayed, begging God to spare my one true love. People started coming to the house. They just kept coming. I stood right by the phone, and each time it rang, I'd pick it up and ask, desperately, "Danny?" Someone called to tell me that the Pentagon had been hit. The phone rang again. It was my brother-in-law. I said, "Danny?"

"No, Kathy," he answered, "It's all over. The North Tower collapsed."

I screamed, "Don't say that! Don't say that!" I was trying to make myself believe that Danny was okay. That he had managed to get out safely.

Deep down, I knew it wasn't possible, but I couldn't face the awful truth. It was unthinkable. Unbearable.

A few minutes later, I received a call from the boys' school. The administration had made an announcement over the intercom about what was happening at the World Trade Center. The assistant principal told me I needed to come get my sons because they were both terrified and screaming.

I tore out the door and down to the school. As soon as I saw my boys I grabbed them and hugged them. The assistant principal told me I needed to keep them quiet and get them out of the school because one of the teachers had a husband in the Towers, too. I was furious. "These are little kids," I said. "Why would you announce this over the intercom? My kids are hysterical because they know that their father is in there, too! And you want them to be quiet?"

I took the boys home and called Jessica. I tried to reassure her, but insisted that she come home right away. I kept telling her he was okay and that he had called. I was trying to convince us both that he would be coming home safely.

The rest of the day was a blur. There were people coming and going constantly. Rumors were spreading throughout the house and through the streets. People were printing out photographs of Danny and whatever else they could to do to help bring him home. I just sat on the couch in the living room and didn't move. I kept the phone on my lap and every time it rang, I would answer it, hoping desperately to hear Danny's voice.

It was near midnight when I went out in the driveway and started vomiting. I felt as if I was having a nervous breakdown, losing all control. My father was there, and I told him, "Daddy, you have to take me to the hospital." He did, but the only thing they could do was give me something to help me sleep. At 5 a.m. the next morning, I approached my dad and said, "Please tell me Danny called." He looked at me, heartbroken, and said, "No."

I refused to accept that my husband was gone. It just wasn't possible. So we formed two groups to go into the city and look for Danny. We had printed hundreds of flyers with his photograph prominently displayed. My group headed toward the downtown area. It was unbelievably quiet and eerie. Nobody was out on the streets. A woman told me that all the Cantor

Fitzgerald people were meeting at the Pierre Hotel. When we arrived, I found Howard Lutnick, the CEO of Cantor Fitzgerald. I tried talking to him, begging him for information about who had gotten out. But he wouldn't tell me anything. He kept insisting that he had to tell everyone what he knew at the same time.

I was frozen with fear as Howard stood up at the microphone and began, "I hate to tell everyone this, but my brother Gary has died. Everyone else who was working at Cantor Fitzgerald . . . they have all died."

It was a knife through my heart. The most horrible thing I could ever have imagined had happened. My Danny was gone.

How will I tell our children? Our godson?

The most gut-wrenchingly difficult thing I have ever had to do is tell my children that their father – the man who was our whole world – was dead. He would never come home again.

I couldn't bear the thought of it. I went to see Terrell first. It took so long to get there, and I was sobbing in the back seat the entire way. I held Terrell in my arms and told him the tragic news. I continued to rock Terrell in my arms for almost an hour as we both cried and held each other close. Terrell cried out, "I love him so much. He was so good to me."

I promised Terrell that I would stay with him until he fell asleep, and eventually he did. I tucked him in his bed, said goodbye to his grandmother, and left.

When I arrived home, I went into the bedroom that I had shared with my husband. Jessica was curled up beside the dresser with a terrified look on her face. I gently told her that her father was gone. Jessica began to scream. I didn't know what else to do except hold her close to me. But she wouldn't let anyone touch her. She cried like I had never heard a person cry before.

On September 13th, I found the courage to tell my precious boys. No mother should ever have to tell their children that their father has been killed. The screaming, wailing, and gagging were horrible. No mother should ever have to see her children in such pain. My own pain meant nothing to me compared to theirs. It was unbearable.

I was now a single, devastated mother with three devastated children. I had absolutely no idea what to do next.

CHAPTER 12

"Now, we have inscribed a new memory alongside those others. It's a memory of tragedy and shock, of loss and mourning. But not only of loss and mourning. It's also a memory of bravery and self-sacrifice, and the love that lays down its life for a friend—even a friend whose name it never knew."

- President George W. Bush, December 11, 2011 -

In the days that followed September 11th, I was tormented by thoughts of how Danny died. He was trapped on the 104th floor of a burning building for more than an hour and a half. I couldn't imagine a more horrifying way to die. The torture was unimaginable, for both of us. It sickened me that he was murdered in a way that was so sadistic, and yet so callous.

Years later, I found a book of 9/11 photographs. Someone had taken photos of the North Tower after it was hit, just before it collapsed. One of the pictures showed people inside the tower pressing against the broken windows, gasping for air. Incredibly, I found a picture that I am quite certain is of Danny. His hands were all black. I have visions of people jumping. It's so hard to watch the visions of 9/11 over and over. But it's part of history and will forever be etched in my mind. I pray that when the building collapsed, he died so quickly that he didn't suffer. However he died I know it was so horrific. I can't bear the thought of him suffering.

I continued to dwell on the irony of both of our sons having one foot out the door the morning of September 11th. My younger son said to me, "Mommy, we'd be dead if you hadn't told us to go back to bed." If it wasn't for the eye affliction and them missing so much school, I would have let them go with their father that fateful day. The pain of losing my husband is unbearable. The thought of losing my husband and my two boys is unthinkable. I don't believe I could have gone on living if that had happened.

My sister and brother-in-law organized an amazing and beautiful memorial service for Danny. The wake was unbelievable. There were photographs of Danny everywhere, and all of his awards and accomplishments were on display. The room was filled with flowers – hundreds and hundreds of flower arrangements. The scent of the flowers was so strong, it reminded me of the scent I had experienced six months before, when I had envisioned Danny's memorial. The scent of funeral flowers surrounded me a few more times during the months that followed. In these moments, I felt that Danny's spirit was lingering beside me.

I was still recovering from my car accident during the wake, so all I could do was just sit in a chair. Long lines of people approached me to express their sympathy, many of them telling me memorable stories about Danny. My sister observed sadly, "Movie stars don't get this kind of reception." The funeral home staff said they had never seen anything like it. All kinds of people came to pay their respects—young and old, rich and poor, people from every imaginable walk of life. It is incredible to see how many lives one human being can touch in just forty years.

Hundreds of children that Danny had coached over the years came, wearing their team jerseys. Years later, they would still talk about how important this man was to them. I have heard that some of them now have tattoos of Danny's name on their bodies. At the service, they passed around a basketball, and those who wanted to speak about Danny stood up to speak when the ball reached them.

The funeral service in the church was incredibly moving. Danny's brother Kevin, an amazing musician, sang during the service. My niece Nikki, who was still a teenager, also sang. She has a gorgeous voice and is just so beautiful, inside and out. They both reminded me so much of Danny. It was the perfect sendoff for a man who was larger than life. "Dan the Man" deserved that. I think he would have felt deeply honored if he could have seen all the people who came to celebrate his life. At the time, I was so overwhelmed that I could hardly take it all in. Later, when I reflected on the memorial service, it filled me with pride and joy.

A few months after the memorial service, a representative of the U.S. Olympic Committee called me to ask if one of my children would like to honor Danny by serving as a runner in the Olympic Torch Relay in New York City. I knew Danny would want Jessica to be the one to participate, and she gladly accepted. She was so excited, but so nervous. In December, our family and close friends gathered at the relay site. When the torch was handed off to Jessica, she started running, and we all ran alongside her. After the final torch was passed to mayor Giuliani, there was a beautiful candle ceremony on the ice at Rockefeller Center to honor those who had lost their lives.

The Olympic Torch Relay was, like the memorial service, an occasion for joy as well as sorrow. It was a special opportunity to honor Danny and celebrate his life. Still, the harsh reality of my family's life without Danny was closing in on us. Things were changing. I was horrified when I looked at a photograph of me taken at the candle ceremony. I looked like a skeleton. I hadn't been able to keep food down for months after Danny's death, and my weight had dropped to under 100 pounds. The day I lost Danny was the beginning of my battle to survive.

CHAPTER 13
Jessica's Perspective: Losing My Father

"I may neither choose who I would, nor refuse who I dislike; so is the will of a living daughter curbed by the will of a dead father."

- *William Shakespeare* -

The last time I saw my father, he was mowing the lawn in the front yard. It was the summer we weren't speaking because of the argument we'd had about my curfew. Summer was coming to a close, so I had to prepare for my return to college. Preseason soccer practice was about to begin. I had returned to my parents' house to pack the rest of my bags. As I crossed the lawn, I marched right past my father without saying a word to him.

A short time later, my mother was injured in a car accident while driving me to college for preseason soccer. Because it was preseason, I couldn't leave, so I called to check on her every day. I would call the house, and every time my father answered, I would hang up the phone immediately. I was just acting like a stubborn brat, because I was not ready to admit I was wrong. One of my close friends on the soccer team knew about my mother's accident and knew that I was refusing to speak to my dad. She convinced me to do the right thing. "Listen to me," she said. "My mom has breast cancer. You never know what could happen. Just talk to your dad."

Later that day, I called, and he answered. I said, "Dad?"

"Hey!" he replied.

It was as if nothing had ever happened.

"How are you doing? I'm coming to your next game (scheduled for September 16th). I can't wait to see you. Your mom is doing all right. Do you want to talk with her?"

I didn't want to talk to her just yet, so I let my father update me on her recovery. I was so grateful to have this conversation with him. I was so grateful that my friend had persuaded me to call him. If I hadn't called, I'm sure the guilt over missing my last opportunity to talk to him would have eaten away at me forever.

September 11th was the first day of my sophomore year of college. The night before, I had gone out with my friends, so I woke up late. I hustled to get to my Business Law class on time. I didn't even turn on the television; I just rushed to class. When I arrived, a close friend asked me, "Why are you here?"

I thought he was joking around with me, so I laughed, "I know, I know. I'm never in class."

"No, Jessica. The World Trade Center was just hit by a plane!" he replied.

It didn't even register that my dad was inside that building, even though my friend reminded me he worked there.

"What do you mean 'a plane'?" I asked, fear growing inside me.

He urged me to leave. All I heard was "A plane ... something happened ... the World Trade Center collapsed. You need to go home, Jess."

My mind went blank as I walked back to my dorm. As I walked into my room the phone began ringing. I answered it and heard my mother's voice. She told me that my father had called her, he was fine, and he was going to make it out. My mother pleaded for me to come home, so she sent a car to pick me up.

Because of the chaos, the bridges in the area were closed, so I had to go to Connecticut and take a ferry to Long Island. I remember thinking as I waited for the ferry, *my dad is athletic, and so he'll make it out.*

When I arrived home, the house was filled with people, and my mother was a mess. All the chaos made me feel panicky. I knew my mother needed the support, but I didn't want to be there. I couldn't bear standing around all these people as they made their sympathetic remarks. No one knew what was going on or whether my father had made it out. We all stood around hoping and praying for the phone to ring.

I wondered where my brothers were, so I went outside to look and found one of my brothers curled up in a chair, sobbing. My youngest brother was upstairs, sitting in a chair and staring at a wall. I felt as if I should get them out of the house, away from all the chaos. I decided to go get my college roommate and take my brothers to Jillian's—an arcade bowling alley.

Unfortunately, there were televisions at Jillian's that replayed the images of the World Trade Center collapsing over and over again. I kept giving my brothers money, and they played all the games they needed to win a gigantic stuffed animal – Sylvester – a gift they could give our father when he came home.

I kept trying to convince myself that my father really was going to come home. I said to myself: *He's athletic. He's only forty years old. He can make it. Yeah, he might not still be in the best shape, but he could still make it down 104 flights of stairs if he needed to.*

The next day, my mother went to the city with a group of people to get information about my father and his coworkers. They were told that no one who worked for Cantor Fitzgerald had made it out. It was the most painful outcome imaginable.

After breaking the news to Terrell, my mother came home to tell me. I remember feeling trapped in my mother's room as she told me what I couldn't bear to hear.

My mother told my brothers, but I couldn't be in the same room while she broke this awful news to them. I don't know how she gathered the strength to tell them the horrible truth. I didn't see my brothers receive this news, but I could hear it. They were only ten and twelve years old. I was nineteen years old, and I couldn't begin wrapping my head around the fact my dad was never coming home. I knew I had to get out of there, even though my aunts tried to keep me from going. I grabbed my belongings, walked out the door, and drove back to my college dorm.

Over the next few days, our friends and relatives tried to find out more about what had happened to my father. They were not ready to give up hope that he had somehow made it out alive, or that maybe his body had been found. They called hospitals and faxed photos of my father. I posted messages on AOL, hoping to hear something – anything – about him. But his body was never found. I was sure he would have been trying to help other people get out of the building – my father wouldn't have just tried to save himself. The body of a man who worked next to my father was eventually found, and it was determined that he had died of smoke inhalation. I hoped that my father went that way too – I imagined that it would feel kind of like going to sleep.

At the memorial service, there were so many people that we had to have a tent set up outside. I think the funeral home had never seen so many people attend a service. At that point, a lot of bridges were still closed, and it wasn't easy to get to Long Island, but people found a way. My mom's sister organized the service because she knows how to get things done (we call her "the general"). My mother was heavily medicated and struggling to keep it together.

The service was a wonderful sendoff for my father, and many people spoke about him. Everyone passed a basketball around the room, and when the ball came to you, it was your turn to speak. My uncle – my mother's brother – delivered a beautiful tribute. He had always idolized my father and captured his spirit perfectly. I didn't want to speak, but my brother and aunt read aloud letters from all three of us siblings. Virtually every child my father had ever coached showed up wearing a team uniform. The Boston Celtics sent my dad's jersey.

After the memorial service, I was sent back to college very quickly – too quickly. I wasn't ready for it. When I walked into my first class – that same Business Law class I was going to on 9/11 – I heard a classmate whisper, "That's the girl whose father died." I turned in my homework and just walked out of the classroom.

I kept up with my schoolwork, but I stopped going to soccer practice for a while. I couldn't watch television because there was constant footage of the Towers collapsing over and over again. Every time I saw those images, it was like I was watching my father die. Sometimes I would cry, but crying didn't make anything better, and I wanted to be strong for my brothers.

Some of my friends were frustrated that I wasn't reaching out to them more. The truth of what happened still hadn't sunk in, and I didn't know what would happen when it finally did. I wondered how I would get through all the holidays and birthdays and anniversaries in the years ahead. I knew that the date my father adopted me would be the hardest.

On 9/11 my dad had planned to take my brothers with him to work, but my parents decided at the last minute that the boys should go to school instead. If my brothers had gone with my dad, I'd be the only surviving family member, because I know my mother wouldn't have been able to go on living. There were other relatives that could have been lost that day, too. One of my uncles was in the Pentagon that day, another uncle was at the White House, and my aunt was on an American Airlines flight.

In 1993, prior to the bombing of the World Trade Center, my father had been offered a job for a company that had offices located in the buildings. He dodged a bullet by declining the job offer. But several years later he accepted the position at Cantor Fitzgerald, so he ended up working at the World Trade Center anyway. It's a painful coincidence that my father and some close friends were planning to leave their jobs at the end of the month to start their own business. *If they would have just made these plans a few weeks sooner, my father would be standing right next to me today.*

I occasionally visited my dad at his office on the 104th floor. He would take me to eat at Windows on the World – a restaurant on the top floor. It took three elevators to get there. During one of my visits, there was a bad storm. The towers were built to sway, and there was a ball on a string, similar to a pendulum, that would swing back and forth when the buildings swayed. I was never afraid of heights, but it was scary to see buildings of this magnitude move the way they did. The thought never made my father fearful. His attitude was always, "If something is going to happen, it will happen. Oh well, live each day!"

Even if the tower hadn't collapsed, my father would not have made it out alive, because his floor was too many levels above the floor that was on fire. We still don't know exactly what happened to him – whether he died of smoke inhalation, jumped from the window, or died when the towers collapsed. Unfortunately, we will never know. It's thinking about the pain and fear he must have been feeling – that's what gets me the most. He was fighting for his life for an hour and a half after the attack. Even though he must have been struggling, he still took the time to call my mother. He knew he had to stay calm for her. I don't know many people that would have the strength to do that. There will never be closure for us, because his body was never recovered. It sometimes feels as if he just vanished into thin air.

In our family, we were taught to not make judgments or stereotype any group of people. Some people blame Muslims for the horror of 9/11, but I am not among them. I do not blame Muslims for murdering my father – extremists murdered my father. I was not brought up to discriminate against a group of people for the actions of certain individuals. Muslims, as a group, were not responsible for my father's death.

I didn't go to Ground Zero right away, and I do not like visiting the site now. I did attend a memorial service a few months after the attacks, and again on the second anniversary. At the two-year anniversary service, my brother read our father's name and I remember feeling violated because people were taking pictures of my brother and me. September 11th affected so many people, tore families apart, and devastated the country. People sometimes compare September 11th to other national tragedies, but I think the pain and trauma is in a category by itself.

The whole world witnessed September 11th and we were all affected by it. In a way, we are all connected by loss, but every person is affected differently. I lost my father, but my mother lost her husband, and my dad's friends lost a beloved companion. None of those relationships can ever be replaced.

The moment the World Trade Centers collapsed, so did my mother. I always say I lost both of my parents that day. I honestly believe that my mother has not experienced one moment of true happiness since my father was murdered. Without her husband, she doesn't know how to be happy again. Her rock is gone . . .

CHAPTER 14

"That though the radiance which was once so bright be now forever taken from my sight. Though nothing can bring back the hour of splendor in the grass, glory in the flower. We will grieve not; rather find strength in what remains behind."

- William Wordsworth -

For a long time after my husband died, I was in a daze. Deep down, I knew I wasn't the Kathy Trant I used to be, but I tried to keep moving forward. I didn't want to give up. When I turned to medical professionals for help, the only thing they could offer me was prescription medication. I often felt over-medicated, and I began drinking more than usual. Most of the time, it felt as if I was drifting out into "la-la land." In retrospect, the medicine only made things worse – it numbed the pain without helping me move past it.

During the months that followed Danny's death I had set a goal – to travel with my children. After the September 11th hijackings, I didn't want my children to be afraid to fly, and I thought it would be best to get on a plane right away. Danny and I had been planning to take the boys to Ireland, where he had lived for five years, but I couldn't face going there without him. Instead, I accepted a friend's invitation to go to Jamaica as a family for Christmas vacation. This would be the first of many family trips over the years.

About six months after Danny died, my mother-in-law called to tell me that Danny's father was near death. I was so sad, and really worried about how the kids would take it.

How much death can they handle?

After everything the children had been through, I knew that taking them to see their grandfather one last time would be the right thing to do. We flew down to Florida to be with my in-laws. The boys understood the reason for the trip, and as I expected, they cried.

After my father-in-law died, Jessica and I flew back down there for the funeral. This was an extremely sad time for us. He was a highly decorated World War II veteran whose medals included two Purple Hearts. He raised nine children and never hesitated to help one more, whether they were related or not. He invited the homeless into his home, fed them, gave them money, helped them find work, and encouraged them to get back on their feet. He was a great example for his children and grandchildren.

Danny loved his father so much, and I was grateful that he did not have to go through the agony of losing his Dad. They had a lot in common – mostly because they both inspired love and devotion from so many people. At the funeral, I remember thinking that now Danny, his father, his nephew, and his brother would all be together. I knew that someday, I would join them all on the other side – the people I had loved and lost.

Unfortunately, these deaths occurred while I was struggling badly. I would take a haphazard cocktail of prescribed medication mixed with alcohol, and then experience full-blown episodes of mania and depression. I realize now that I was suffering from post-traumatic stress disorder, or PTSD. I didn't realize at the time that stress could activate my bipolar disorder. It had been dormant for so long because Danny had helped me manage my mood swings and think positive. Only Danny could do that for me.

For about a year, I became like a hermit. I turned my back on all of my old friends and acquaintances. I felt so angry, and I just couldn't stand to see anybody who had been part of my life before I lost Danny. I couldn't bear to see others happy while I felt lost and alone. For a while, I couldn't even bear to be with my family. Leaving the boys in the care of my mother and Jessica, I spent a lot of time with a New York City firefighter. He had been there to help save lives on September 11th, and being with him made me feel connected to Danny.

I feel terrible about what my children went through. I dug myself a hole and buried myself in it for a long time. Jessica and my mother were there to support me, no matter what I did. Jessica also had to take on responsibility for parenting her little brothers – everything from supervision to discipline. This forced Jessica to grow up too fast. Jessica and I have always been, and remain, extremely close. But I carry a lot of guilt about the burdens she had to carry at such a young age.

Jessica not only stepped in as a mother figure to her brothers, but also to me, her own mother. I was unable to eat for months, which brought me down to 85 pounds. Jessica convinced me to try drinking nutritional supplements when I couldn't keep my food down. At one point, she was so concerned for my heath that she took a photograph of me and made me look at it every day. Seeing how dangerously thin I had become was quite an eye opener.

She was a great support system, pushing me to move past the tragedy. But I wasn't the only one suffering. Jessica suffered because of me. She would tell me, "You don't know what it's like to hear your mother crying herself to sleep every night. You don't know what it's like having a mother who's on a downward spiral and wants to kill herself. You don't know what it's like to have a mother who's not the same mom anymore. We want our mother back! The one who was a class mom, who made dinner, who did everything for our family."

Though my heart went out to my daughter, I knew I could never give her what she was asking for. I would never be the same mother or the same person again. All I could do was try my best to go on.

With Danny gone, it was up to me to handle the family's finances – something I'd never done before. I'd never paid a bill during our marriage. At the time of Danny's death, he had worked his way up the corporate ladder and was finally making a sizeable salary. After his death, I received a substantial bonus from his company, as well as benefits from his life insurance policy. Eventually, I would also be eligible for money from the 9/11 Victims Compensation Fund. In the meantime, private donations for our family poured in from friends, coworkers, acquaintances, and even strangers. I was so grateful for the support, but all the money was overwhelming. Managing finances had never been my responsibility, and I made many bad decisions. Even though those decisions were driven by inexperience and grief, they would come back to haunt me later.

Nine months before Danny was murdered, we bought our first house together. We had plans to make significant improvements to it, because it was important to us to provide a comfortable home for our children. When Danny died, I didn't want to leave our home – the memories we had made there were good ones, and I wanted to remain where we had been so happy. I decided that renovating our home would be a way to honor Danny's memory and create a welcoming space where our kids could grow up.

When Danny died, we had been in the process of getting rid of the black mold we had discovered growing in the basement. It was undermining the value of our property and posed a serious health hazard to our sons. It was an expensive process – the entire house had to be almost gutted – but once the mold was removed, the boys' eye problems improved almost immediately.

Renovating the house was a huge project – far bigger than I imagined at first. My goal was to create a happy home where all the neighborhood kids and all my children's friends could gather and have fun. After making sure every bit of the mold was removed, I expanded the house to make it big enough to accommodate our family and friends comfortably. During the course of the renovation, I discovered that I had a creative flair for interior design. Decorating the rooms was very therapeutic for me. I felt energized and it strengthened my will to live.

I came up with themes for different rooms. The family room had an American theme, with a red, white and blue palette. There were denim sofas and cherry leather chairs. The kitchen was renovated to accommodate a huge table everyone could gather around. All the rooms were homey and welcoming – I didn't want anything so formal that people wouldn't feel comfortable hanging out there.

My vision for the house was realized. The kids loved it, and were always inviting friends over. Our first party was a huge one – we opened it up to all the people in our village who had supported us, to thank them for their kindness. More than 150 people came to our house that night, and everyone had a great time.

Another goal I set was to broaden the education of my children through travel opportunities. I wanted them to see the world and be exposed to different cultures. I also hoped that traveling together would help us all heal by keeping us close as we explored new places together. When Danny died, so many people reached out to provide emotional support, and I will be forever grateful for that. But one of the biggest challenges was getting back to normal, everyday life. I thought travel would ease the pain of that transition and help us move forward as a family.

During the years that followed, we took many trips, and saw a great deal of the world. Of course, even the excitement of travel couldn't take away the trauma and grief of losing a husband and a father. I remained emotionally unstable, which was hard on my children. Some trips were more successful than others. But looking back, I think that it was through travel that we all bonded the most. It was a wonderful shared experience.

One trip in particular was quite memorable because it deepened my connection to Danny. We were in Croatia, where my friend Diane had a home. She and I decided to go to Mejugorje, a town in Bosnia that is famous for apparitions of the Blessed Mother. As we were waiting in line at the church, I opened my Bible at random, and saw that it was the book of Daniel. There was a special statue of Jesus there, and I touched the Bible to the statue.

As we entered the church, Diane said, "We can listen to the service, but it's always in different languages, never in English." But that day it was in English, and the scripture reading was from the Book of Daniel. Coincidentally, the priest's sermon was about the way people came together to support one another after the September 11th attacks on America. As I listened to him speak, I found myself wishing that people could be that supportive of one another all the time, not just during a crisis.

Another trip that was special to me was our visit to the Vatican while we were in Rome. We admired all of the beautiful art, and I offered up many prayers for Danny. The taxi drivers seemed to play Italian music constantly, but the instant we got into this cab, an American song came on the radio. It was Danny's and my wedding song, which I hadn't heard in years. We all just sat there in shock, listening to the words: *"Atlantic Star Girl, you are to me all that a woman can be ..."* I felt so loved, and I felt like Danny was telling me everything was going to be okay.

In 2003, my family had to meet with Kenneth Feinberg, who served as the Special Master for the 9/11 Victims Compensation Fund. He was responsible for determining the amount that each victim or victim's family would receive. I am grateful for the funds we received, but I found the process itself demeaning. The lawyers had to prepare a thousand-page inquiry to set a value on my husband's life. My children and I had to sit down with this man we didn't know – who didn't know Danny – and tell him what we thought Danny was worth. Of course, there was no way that any amount of money could replace my husband, the father of my children, who was trapped in a burning building and murdered.

The whole experience was upsetting and deeply offensive. The report contained personal details like "Mrs. Trant called her husband twenty times a day. She was dependent on him for everything." The statement may have been accurate, but it didn't begin to capture the essence of our relationship. Danny and I stayed in touch with each other constantly because that was how our relationship functioned. I was dependent on him for some things, but there were also ways in which he was dependent on me. We complemented each other in many ways.

I felt vulnerable because I had no financial skills or knowledge to draw on in this situation. In order to be eligible for the funds, I had to sign away some of my rights, giving me no legal recourse in the future. But there was no guarantee that I would receive as much as a single dollar in return. Sometimes I think it would have been better for the Victims Compensation Fund to give all the families the same amount. I was astonished that they wanted me to put a price tag on my husband.

By 2005 I was managing to function, but I was still emotionally unstable. The medications I was on weren't helping. In fact, they suppressed my inhibitions, and I had no impulse control.

I developed an addiction to shopping. Shopping was my "fix." Somehow, it made me feel good about myself. At first I didn't recognize the signs, but I had a problem. People often use the term "shopaholic" in a joking way, but it's truly an addiction, and it's nothing to laugh about. As I became more self-aware about my compulsive spending, I felt sorry for others who suffered from the same addiction. I thought about all the people struggling to make ends meet and ending up in debt for the rest of their lives.

During this time, I made one of the biggest mistakes of my life. I agreed to an interview with a reporter from a newspaper I assumed was a legitimate publication. I was unaware that the newspaper was widely known as a sensationalist tabloid. My understanding was that the article the reporter would write would address my experiences as a 9/11 widow in a respectful way.

I should never have agreed to that interview. Overmedicated and struggling with PTSD and bipolar disorder, I was not in my right mind. I was weak, vulnerable, and ripe for exploitation. I remember naively thinking the interview would provide an opportunity for me to not only share my personal journey since Danny's death, but to help raise public awareness about the true nature of shopping addictions.

The article presented me in an extremely negative light – a pathetic parody of myself. They had manipulated me into revealing details about my personal finances, and the reporter included a long list of my admittedly extravagant, and often eccentric, expenditures. He milked them for all they were worth, and the article exaggerated the amount of money I received from public sources and private donations.

I was devastated. So was Jessica, and we were both furious. She called up the reporter and screamed, "How could you do this to my mother?

You took all these things out of context and made her out to be a horrible person. All she wanted to do was help people."

Even before the article was published, I had heard that some people were spreading nasty rumors about the way I spent money. I was actually quite confused by the rumors. I tried to give my children a safe, happy home and opportunities to travel, and I thought the public would view those activities as worthwhile – even admirable – investments.

To this day, I stand by those decisions. Renovating my house was necessary for health reasons, and refurbishing the house helped keep me grounded. Plus, I "paid it forward" by opening my new home up for other people to enjoy. The travel broadened my children's knowledge and kept our family together. It also kept me sane, in many ways.

The article was just the first step in a media nightmare. Journalists and television producers who had seen the tabloid article about the "Crazy 9/11 Widow" hounded me for follow-up interviews. Everyone wanted a piece of me. In an effort to make things better, I agreed to some of these interviews, but they just seemed to make things worse.

When Jessica and I were invited to appear on the *Oprah Winfrey Show*, we thought that maybe, at last, someone would give us a fair hearing. We believed this would be an opportunity to set the record straight by sharing the truth of our own experiences. However, the whole tone of the interview was confrontational; I felt judged instead of heard. Jessica and I were both disappointed.

The negative publicity continued for months, growing more and more hateful. I felt as if I was the face of September 11th stupidity. People snidely accused me of loving my "fifteen minutes of fame." I was sickened and disgusted by one commentator who characterized 9/11 widows as greedy vultures who smiled while their husbands burned. Instead of seeing me for the flawed and wounded person I was, people talked about me as if I was a murderer. I just couldn't understand it. I wasn't a monster. And I was never one to condemn other people for their weaknesses. At heart, I was just a simple girl who never wanted anything but my husband, my kids, and a nice home for my family.

By this point, I had come to agree with the adage that money is the root of all evil. On the one hand, the financial support I received provided my family with security and opportunities that I truly appreciated. On the other hand, the money I received became a weapon that people used against me.

I now thought of the money I received from the Victims Compensation Fund as blood money. Danny and I were such proud people, and we worked hard for everything we had. It had made me feel so small to sit there with my children like I was begging for money.

I felt like just giving back the individual donations I had received. Eventually, I did try to give away a comparable amount, donating to a variety of individuals and charitable organizations. But people seemed so angry with me for the decisions I had made. Whenever I gave a gift to someone, it never occurred to me that I should dictate how that gift was used. So I couldn't understand why people were so judgmental about my choices.

I'd ask myself: *Why would you give a person a gift and then make the person feel guilty about it?*

I wouldn't.

If I had it to do all over again, I never would have taken money from anyone. It allowed me to take care of my family's material needs, but it didn't buy happiness. And it couldn't take away the huge loss we had all experienced.

All the negative publicity made me feel so ashamed, and I blamed myself for what had happened. I thought maybe if I had just kept my mouth shut, this humiliating storm of public criticism never would have happened. But I've always had that problem. I don't know how to filter what I say. When Danny was by my side, he would save me from myself. After reminding me to rein myself in, he would remind me it was not a big deal and we would laugh together. But Danny wasn't there anymore.

After 9/11, I was humbled by people's generosity. I can never thank them enough for their gifts of love and support as well as their financial gifts. I'm sorry if those people feel that I've let them down. I admit I made mistakes, so many mistakes. But it wasn't my intention to be ungrateful or disrespectful or malicious. When I renovated my house or took my children on trips or bought things, I certainly wasn't doing it out of spite. I never meant to hurt anyone.

The negative media frenzy came at a time when I was still very fragile. Over the next few years, I slipped into a downward spiral of self-destructive behaviors. Every time I tried to work my way back up, I'd get slammed by another body blow and sink even further into alcohol, drugs, and despair.

In 2006, I had just returned from a trip overseas when my mother called. She said, "I don't want you to panic, but your sister Mary is in the hospital, and I don't think she's going to make it."

I was distraught. "Mom, what are you saying?" I was screaming. Mary was my little sister, and I couldn't imagine anything bad happening to her. She was only thirty-four, the youngest of my mother's children. She was born on Christmas day, and was always happy-go-lucky, talking about peace and love. She was an amazing artist and just loved everything that life had to offer.

I immediately drove to the hospital, terrified that something awful was actually happening. It was. Sepsis was taking over her body, and the doctors said that her hands and feet would have to be amputated. I knew that if that had happened, she wouldn't have wanted to go on living. When I saw her in the hospital, I whispered in her ear, "Just go to heaven, Mary."

A few days later she died, breaking all of our hearts once again. The most devastating part of the whole ordeal was seeing how it affected my mother. No parent should ever have to say goodbye to their own child. It is one of the worst heartbreaks a person can endure.

A few years after Mary's death I awoke one day to the horrible, familiar sound of someone wailing. It was Jessica. I ran to her and found her doubled over, screaming that my brother Chris was dead. Chris was my half-brother – my birth father's son – and I was quite close to him. He had been like a surrogate father to my kids after Danny died. In fact, the day he died in his sleep, Chris was scheduled to take my son to the Kentucky Derby. This was a huge blow to all of us, but especially to Chris' two beautiful young sons. Once again, I witnessed my loved ones – this time my father and stepmother – experience the gut-wrenching grief of losing a child. It was horrific.

Each one of these losses took a tremendous toll on all of us, but I seemed to be the one who had the most trouble coping. I remember being so out of it after Mary's death that I once rubbed my skin raw while using a pumice stone. I didn't even realize what I was doing. My brother in law, my nephew, my husband, my father in law, my sister and then my brother.

How much can a family take?

At the time, I was also having pain from rheumatoid arthritis, and the doctor gave me a prescription for Vicodin. The moment I swallowed that first pill, I was addicted. After about six months, I was up to fourteen Vicodin pills a day.

The children were older, but still needed a mother's supervision. Lucy and Anna, my housekeepers and trusted friends, were there to help out. They were always there to help out around the house and made sure the boys were never home alone.

Meanwhile, my downward spiral continued. I started dating a guy who could get me drugs. We were perfect for each other – two drug addicts, going nowhere. After about a year, I somehow found the strength to break up with him. But he was not pleased, and his anger exploded in violence.

One day I was sitting in my car, about to start the engine, when a fist suddenly shattered the window next to me. This ex-boyfriend had punched it out. Glass went everywhere – even in my eyes.

It took hours for the plastic surgeon to remove all the broken glass from my face. When I woke up, my face was covered in stitches and I had two black eyes. Lucy was in one chair, and Anna was in the other. Lucy said, "Kathy, you're going to be mad at us. We know who did this to you. We called Jessica, and she called the police."

At first, I lied to the police because I was terrified of what my ex-boyfriend might do next. But the police officers said that if I didn't tell them who had assaulted me, they would arrest me. I told the truth about the broken window, and then I went into court to file a restraining order. I hoped that it was finally over.

In 2009, I hit rock bottom. My sons had graduated from high school and gone off to college, and I became even more depressed. One day when I was home alone, I felt surrounded by nothing but loneliness. It was unbearable, and I wanted it to end. I wrapped a belt around my neck and attached the belt to the showerhead. I don't know how long I hung there. I became aware of my girlfriend near me, holding me up. She somehow got the belt off my neck, laid me on the bed, and called the police. I was screaming and wailing, and when the police arrived, I fought them so hard that they had to handcuff me to get me into an ambulance.

I was hospitalized for two weeks until the doctors determined that I was no longer a danger to myself. After I was released, I was treated as an outpatient and had to check in at the psychiatric ward every day. I was still very depressed and spent many of the ensuing months in bed.

When my stepmother – my father's wife – learned about my suicide attempt, she said, "Kathy could you imagine how we would have felt if you had killed yourself, if you had done that to us?"

Before this point in my life, I had never been able to understand why a person would even consider suicide. But I finally understood how incredibly painful life can be for some people. At the same time, I realized how selfish it had been for me to attempt suicide – especially after my mother and father and stepmother had experienced the death of another child.

After my suicide attempt, I was officially diagnosed with PTSD and bipolar disorder. When I subsequently moved back to Massachusetts, I finally found a wonderful therapist, Joy Gosselin. For years I had been moving from therapist to medical professional back to therapist, but nothing had really helped until I found Joy. She saved my life.

I had tried many times on my own to eliminate drugs from my life, going cold turkey and flushing the pills down the toilet. I just couldn't do it without the right kind of support. I was finally on the right medication and my healing process had begun.

Joy helped me come to terms with all the pain and grief in my life. When Danny was with me, he had kept my life in balance, but after he was murdered, life became overwhelming. Without him in my life, I was assailed from all sides – by my own brain chemistry, as trauma triggered my bipolar disorder; by my past, with its burden of sexual and physical abuse; and by society, with its judgmental attitudes.

Joy also helped me deal with the secondary trauma of the scathing media coverage. I'd always been hypersensitive to other people's opinions, and I was devastated by the media's portrayal of me. Through therapy, I learned to put that experience in perspective.

My therapist said, "It's okay. You made a mistake. You shouldn't have talked to that reporter, but you did, and this is what happened to you. So what? Move on. You were hurt by it and wish it never happened, but it is what it is. And it's over and done with now."

It wasn't surprising to me that some people disapproved of me. But I came to understand that I didn't have to feel intimidated by that small percentage of people who tried to put me down. Instead, I could view their hurtful behavior as the actions of silly, immature people. I vowed not to let them hurt me anymore, though it wasn't easy.

There have been many times that I wished *I* had been the one to die on 9/11 instead of Danny. I have often worried that Danny would be disappointed in me and how I handled his death and the aftermath. I do think he would be angry that I tried to commit suicide – he would be horrified that I would hurt our family so deeply. I confided in Jessica that I thought he would have been a much better parent. Jessica urged me not to say that, but I still believed it.

But in my heart, I knew how much Danny loved me. He believed in me and had my back no matter what anybody else thought. I am certain that he would be proud that I kept looking until I found the help I needed to recover. I know he would be proud that our three children are all college graduates and good – even wonderful – human beings. We were completely in sync about our love for them, in life and in death. Last of all, I know Danny would be proud that I finally got strong enough to stick up for myself and move on.

CHAPTER 15
Jessica's Perspective: Life without My Father

"My father gave me the greatest gift anyone could give another person, he believed in me."

- Jim Valvano -

D uring the months after 9/11, my mother was a wreck. She couldn't eat and was wasting away. Her face was sunken in, and she looked twenty years older than her actual age. She didn't understand how horrible she looked. When she looked in a mirror, all she saw was a person in mourning. I showed her a photograph of herself and said, "Look at you. You're a skeleton."

Before 9/11, my mother was like June Cleaver – that perfect mother on the 1950s television series *Leave It to Beaver*. She was the best mom ever – fixing nice dinners every night and constantly giving us hugs. After 9/11 everything was different. Our family routines fell apart. She didn't want to do anything that reminded her of the life we had lost. Once in a while she would make dinner, but it was hard for all of us to look at that empty chair at the end of the table.

My mother didn't seem to know how to be a mother anymore and she didn't know how to make it better. She just bought us things, which gave us some momentary pleasure. I had to be the one to discipline the boys. My father had always played that role in the past because she didn't want to be the bad guy.

For the first year after 9/11, my mother was physically there, but emotionally absent. When she started spending time with a New York City firefighter, she got my full wrath. I was so angry.

Why in the world would she want to be with another man?

I couldn't understand until later, when I took a step back and thought about it. I realized that she wasn't trying to replace my father. She was so in love with her husband that she had grown desperate to connect with someone. Anyone.

The firefighter was a good person, but of course that poor guy didn't stand a chance. There was no way he was going to live up to my dad. My mother was constantly talking about her husband, and it didn't help that she had this nineteen-year-old daughter going for the guy's throat.

After 9/11, when the initial outpouring of support started to subside, I think my mother felt abandoned. Of course, during a crisis, people say, "We'll be there for you, whatever you need," but eventually they have to go back to their own lives. My mother was heartbroken. Her world had been turned upside down, so when people started disappearing, she got angry.

I've handled my grief differently than my mom handled hers. She finds comfort in sharing her grief, in talking about her loss, and it helps her to be surrounded by supportive people. I cry in private and I don't like to be touched or hugged when I'm grieving. That's just how I do things. I even get uncomfortable when people express sympathy. When they say, "Oh, I'm so sorry," I don't know what to say back—*thank you?* And I didn't want that look people give you – the pitying look.

The first day I went back to class and heard the other students whispering about me, I thought to myself, "Oh, my God. Now I'm always going to be known as that girl who lost her dad on 9/11." I didn't want to be a poster child. I just moved away from everyone emotionally at that point.

After my father was killed, I stopped sleeping. I've had severe insomnia for over a decade. At first I was taking strong sleeping pills, since my mother made sure that all of us saw a psychiatrist. Mine gave me Ambien and Zoloft – didn't even want to hear my story, just handed me the drugs. That psychiatrist was a piece of work. I was nineteen years old at the time. Needless to say, I stopped seeing that doctor and switched to Tylenol PM.

The only activity that engaged me was watching the Food Network channel. The shows were different back then – instead of featuring cooks like Rachel Ray, they featured accomplished chefs like Emeril and Bobby Flay. Unable to sleep, I'd watch the cooking shows and infomercials all night long. My college friends understood. They would come and check on me, but they didn't push. They understood that I didn't want to talk about it until I felt ready. I didn't want to be at college, so every weekend I went home to make sure everything was all right.

Witnessing my mother's grief wore me down. She's always been a crier, and I was used to that. I remember one time when my dad and I were playing gin rummy, and my mother came into the room, crying hysterically. We were like, "Who died?!" As it turned out, she had just been reading a sad novel – *Bridges of Madison County*. But I had never seen her cry the way she cried after 9/11. It was soul shattering.

For a while, I kept trying to help my mother. I read up on how to help people who are suffering from grief and trauma. But then I'd go home and see her wasting away, and I saw that she didn't have any will to go on. That made me feel helpless and trapped, so I stopped coming home. That was probably one of my weakest moments. I'm not proud of it, but I just couldn't handle things anymore

Hearing your mother cry every single time you call her is hard to bear. Sometimes she would say to me, "I don't want to live anymore. I wish I had died instead of your dad. He would be such a better parent."

I have a brash personality and always speak my mind, which sometimes gets me into trouble. I don't sugarcoat things. If you ask me a question, I'm going to give you my truth. And if you've pissed me off, I'll let you know about it. But I hate feeling vulnerable, and I don't like people to see that side of me. Losing my father on 9/11 was frightening and made me afraid of getting close to anyone else. I just completely closed myself off.

I had been living with my boyfriend, but pushed him away, fighting him off when he tried to reach me. I had seen what loss was like. I had seen how much my mother loved my father, and I saw what it did to her when she lost him. That fear of losing my loved ones has stayed with me to this day. When my beloved dog died last year, it just about destroyed me.

Before my father died, my parents were planning to invest in their house by remodeling it. After 9/11, when black mold was discovered in the basement, renovation was no longer an option. The whole house was gutted, and my mother redesigned it from the ground up, making decisions about every little detail, from the molding to the grout. It turned out that she had a real talent for interior design – a kind of spatial intelligence. There was an interior design teacher who told her, "You're a savant. You were never trained to do this, but you still do it far better than most people."

During the years after 9/11, my mother took my brothers and me on trips all over the world. We went on an amazing safari in Africa, riding ATVs in areas with all kinds of wildlife. Once we stayed in a hut that had an outdoor shower. While I showered, I literally could hear hippos groaning nearby.

One trip that was special to me was our trip to South Africa. When I was a little girl, I saw the movie *Jaws* and became obsessed with sharks. I remember my father going to the library with me to help me find books on sharks. Reading about them was both terrifying and fascinating. So I had always wanted to go on one of those expeditions where you can swim with Great White Sharks in the wild. I persuaded my mother to take my brother and me to South Africa for one of those expeditions. I even persuaded her to participate in the dive. At first she was like, "No way I'm doing that." But then she ended up being the first one in the water.

I looked around and asked, "Where's Mom?"

And she called out, "I'm in the cage!" She was the first one to dive, and she stayed underwater for forty-five minutes.

I felt good about getting my mother to step outside her comfort zone. I tried to lead by example. On another trip, I actually succeeded in getting her to jump out of an airplane, when we went skydiving together.

Several years after 9/11 my mother came under attack for the ways she spent money. The Victims Compensation Fund provided a lump sum, but first my mother had to give a 1000-page deposition about her husband. She had to explain not only how much he contributed financially but also what kind of person he was, going into every little detail. Our family also received many generous individual donations, but there was a real backlash later. The way I see it, a gift is a gift; after you give something away, it's no longer yours. But it seems to be human nature to want to control how a gift is used. There were people who disapproved of the way my mother used money they had given her, and they did not hesitate to criticize her publicly.

My mother was totally unprepared to handle family finances, because she had never paid the bills or balanced the checkbook. I wasn't much better at managing money, myself. So it's true that we both ended up being careless with our money and making frivolous expenditures, and my mother developed a shopping addiction. In addition to being exploited by the media, my mother was taken advantage of by people who profited from her generosity. There were some people who were more than willing to let her pick up the tab.

After she was raked over the coals by the media, my mother went downhill fast. She became addicted to illegal drugs and got involved with an unsavory man who was also a drug addict. The low point came when my mother's housekeepers called to tell me that my mother was hurt and that her boyfriend was responsible. He had smashed her car window and beat her up.

My mother was going to let him get away with it. She was afraid of him, so she was planning to say that a stranger attacked her. I was so angry I could hardly control it. I insisted that she file an accurate police report, and I set up a three-way telephone conversation to ensure that she went through with it.

I just couldn't understand how she could have allowed a man to do that to her. She had always taught me to be a strong, independent woman. If I hadn't been there to stop her, I honestly think she would have just gone back to him. She would have reverted to a pattern established earlier in her life, before she met my father. Just like the lowlife who beat her up when she was most vulnerable.

The full extent of her injuries from the assault was not apparent for some time. The trauma to her eye bothered her for months. And nearly a year after the attack, she said, "I feel like there's something in my forehead." When she returned to the plastic surgeon for a consult, he ended up pulling a big piece of broken glass out of her forehead.

Even though she broke up with the man who assaulted her, my mother was still in bad shape. When I'd try to talk to her, she would just stare into space. I would look into her crystal blue eyes and feel like I was looking all the way through them, to the back of her head; it was like there was nothing there. That was really scary.

Though my mother sought medical help, I felt that she deliberately chose doctors who would coddle her. In my opinion, what she needed was someone to be firm with her. Her situation made me think of that show *The Biggest Loser*. There are two trainers on that show—one coddles the contestants, but the other is bluntly honest and really gets in their faces. I thought my mother needed a doctor who would give her a dose of reality.

In 2009 my mother became very depressed and tried to take her own life. At the time, I was dealing with a lot of stress. When my grandmother called to tell me that my own mother had just tried to kill herself, I've never been angrier with my mother in my entire life.

She was hospitalized for a long time because she wouldn't admit that she tried to hurt herself, even though she had been found hanging from a belt around her neck. It was during her stay in the hospital that she was diagnosed with bipolar disorder. Before my dad died, she had some mood swings, but not very often. But after 9/11 the mood swings were really intense. One moment she would be crying inconsolably; then a moment later, she was laughing hysterically.

When that would happen, I would sometimes say, "Mom, you're bipolar." I'd done some research and knew that those extreme highs and lows were not normal.

But when I told her that, she just thought I was putting her down.

"Mom," I said, "I'm not trying to be negative. I'm saying you really are bipolar. I looked it up."

So I wasn't surprised the day my mother was diagnosed. The doctor said, "We have a diagnosis. Do you want your daughter to be in the room?"

She said, "Yeah, absolutely. I don't want to hide anything from her."

The doctors reported that my mother was suffering from post-traumatic stress disorder as well as bipolar disorder. They explained that a traumatic event can exacerbate bipolar symptoms, making the highs higher and the lows lower. That description certainly fit my mother. Before my father died, she was eccentric, but after 9/11 her moods were like a violent roller coaster. I read somewhere that the worst thing you can do for someone with bipolar disorder is give them the wrong medications. Some drugs for depression will actually worsen bipolar symptoms. For years, my mother had been taking various prescriptions that were not helping.

In general, I believe that doctors rely too heavily on prescription drugs to treat emotional and psychological problems. But when people suffer from a chemical imbalance, it's important to find the proper medication to address the problem. For people like my mother, who also abuse illegal drugs, treatment becomes more complicated.

After she was released from the hospital, my mother still faced a long road to recovery. At first, she was still seeing doctors who were ineffectual at best, doctors who seemed to enable her dysfunctional behaviors rather than eliminate them.

When I think about my mother's struggles – and my own – over the past twelve years, I sometimes wonder how we'll ever come to terms with the loss of my father. My mother finds some comfort going to Ground Zero, but I don't find peace there. I don't like it at all. I feel like the media glamorizes the site, and there are always so many people there taking pictures.

The last time I went to Ground Zero with my mother was the ten-year anniversary of 9/11. There was a group of protestors claiming that the American government was responsible for the attack.

Why couldn't you have protested on another day? Why are you doing this on a day when the families of 9/11 victims are here? We didn't do anything to you.

I think my mother also finds some peace in her spiritual beliefs. Though my parents raised their kids Catholic, they didn't force their beliefs on us. They just said, "This is what we believe. But here's the world— believe what you want." One of my brothers is interested in religion, but the other is more scientific, like I am. Even though I'm not religious myself, I don't discriminate against people for their religious beliefs. I can see how religion gives people hope – if you believe in God and heaven, then you have hope that death is not the end.

My mother looks for spiritual signs in the physical world. She was especially struck by one event that nobody has been able to explain. My parents had a thing for red roses. Every Valentine's Day, my father would give my mother red roses. In 2000, when my parents bought our house, they wanted to plant some roses. Because the house was painted yellow, they decided to plant a yellow rosebush in the front yard.

One day I was helping my brother learn how to take a pill for his juvenile rheumatoid arthritis. My mother was no help; she gets upset whenever her children have to do anything uncomfortable. So I told her to get out of the house. We live near a beach, so she agreed to take a walk. A short while later, my mother suddenly burst into the house and cried, "Oh my God, you have to come outside and see the rosebush!"

So we all went outside to look at the yellow rosebush in the front yard. Near the bottom of the bush, three yellow roses were in bloom. But all the other roses blooming on the bush were bright red. This had never happened before. And nobody had ever seen anything like it.

Even though I'm not religious, I do believe that everything happens for a reason. I always told people that you have to find the silver lining in everything. I can't make sense of my dad dying when he did and the way he did, but his passing did give me an opportunity to be more involved in my brothers' lives. So there's one silver lining.

Despite all that's happened, my mother and I are still close, still two peas in a pod. This book is more hers than mine, and I hope that it brings her some closure. I hope that she feels at peace about passing along my father's legacy. I guess love is always a double-edged sword. That's why my mother needed to tell the whole story, the loss as well as the love. My father gave us so much love and happiness that losing him almost destroyed us, but nothing can take away our memories of him.

After 9/11, I got a tattoo on my wrist that says, "Live for the Day." My father's life was relatively short. He used to joke around and say, "I'm not living past forty. When I turn forty, you can just push me off the Empire State Building." As it turned out, his fortieth birthday was, in fact, his last, but he still lived such a full life. I love to tell stories about my dad. He really did have a larger-than-life personality. I talk about him all the time, keeping the stories alive. I don't talk about him being gone. Instead, I focus on the little things – the funny things he would say and do, the songs he would sing. And I feel grateful, but I miss him. And I will miss him every day – every moment – for the rest of my life.

CHAPTER 16
In Honor of Danny

"I've never tried to block out the memories of the past, even though some are painful. I don't understand people who hide from their past. Everything you live through helps to make you the person you are now."

- Sophia Loren -

Danny Trant was not your typical person – nothing about him was average. Even though he only lived to be 40 years old, he touched literally thousands of peoples' lives. It's not an exaggeration to say that everyone who knew him loved him. He cared so much for his family and friends. After 9/11 there were many tributes to Danny, including Jessica running the Olympic torch in his honor, two state legislatures honoring him, and his hometown naming January 2nd as "Dan Trant Day." Another town built a gymnasium in his honor – the Dan Trant Memorial Gym. Newspapers published articles praising his character and achievements.

Most importantly, thousands of people wrote letters after 9/11 to express their admiration for Danny. I received so many beautiful letters. The letters are the most important part of this effort to capture Danny's life, because they provide so much insight into how special Danny was and how much people loved him.

The letters started pouring in immediately after 9/11 and continued to arrive for months. All kinds of people wrote – adults, children, friends, relatives, current and former colleagues, fellow athletes, acquaintances, and even strangers. Some of the letters were read aloud at Danny's memorial service.

Many of the people who wrote had known Danny when he was young and had never forgotten him. I received one letter from a priest saying what a great altar boy Danny was. I also read letters from his teachers commenting on what a wonderful student he was. In another letter, a girl who was his classmate explained how Danny was the only one who befriended her when she moved to town. The other kids picked on her, and he told them to stop. So they did.

Today, Danny's sons and daughter are just like he was – kind to everyone they meet. In my mind, Danny was a man's man – the best possible role model for what a man should be. You can tell from the letters how much other men loved and admired him. If every man would strive to be like Danny, the world would be a better place.

I want to include some examples of the letters I received. They are an inspiration to me to be a better person and live my life as Danny lived his life. Take each day and live it to the fullest. I am happy to say I love life today. It was a long, hard road to get to this place. But I can look back and say "I am the luckiest woman alive to have had Dan Trant in my life. He truly was my soul mate."

EPILOGUE

When life held troubled times, and had me down on my knees, there's always been someone, to come along and comfort me. A kind word from a stranger, to lend a helping hand, a phone call from a friend, just to say, I understand. But ain't it kind of funny, at the dark end of the road, that someone lights the way, with just a single ray of hope.

-Excerpt from "Angels Amongs Us" -
- Artist: Alabama -

D anny Trant was the love of my life. He was my world – my *everything*. Before I met him, I was a bird with broken wings. I was frequently challenged by unfortunate events and my fears nearly destroyed me. When I met Danny, he mended my broken wings and made me whole again. He helped me believe that I could do anything – I could fly.

On September 11, 2001, my husband was murdered at his workplace in the World Trade Center. When I lost him, my life crumbled around me, and there I was again, broken in such a profound way, I didn't think I could ever be whole again.

The love Danny and I shared was a rare and beautiful thing. But it wasn't just me he transformed. Danny reached out to so many other people, and their lives, like mine, were made better by his presence.

Generations from now, I want this book to remain in the world, even if it's just sitting on a shelf collecting dust. Danny has passed, but I want his legacy to live forever on this earth. He made a difference. His family, his friends, his coworkers, the children he coached, myself, our children – everyone he came in contact with, he changed.

It has taken me a long time to find the strength to recollect how dramatically my life and the lives of those around me have changed since 9/11. It has also taken me a great deal of time to find the courage to, once again, put myself in the public's eye. This is a painful place for me, but I want to shine a light on Danny's life. Since I knew him in a way that nobody else did, this has become my mission. It's one small thing I can do for a man who did so much for me – for everyone.

Through all of my misfortunes, including this most horrible tragedy, I have learned the most important lesson—to overcome loss and embrace hope.

This is for you, Danny.

Daniel Patrick Trant

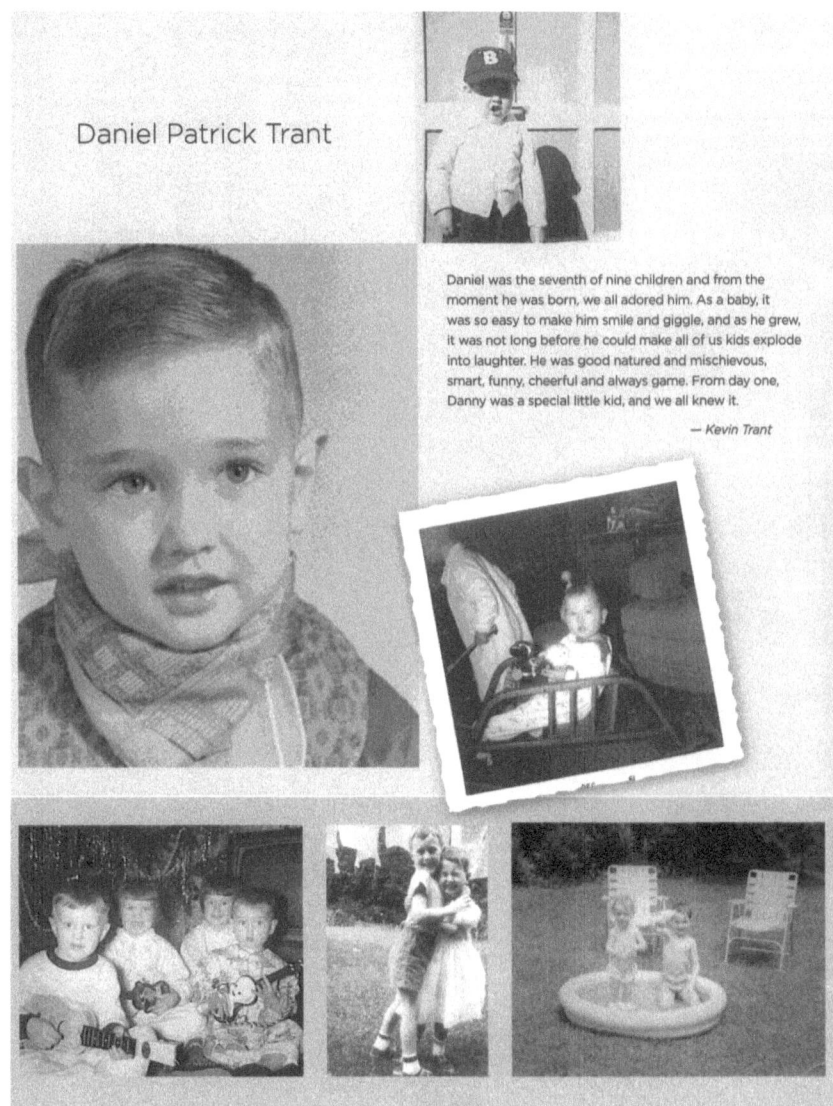

Daniel was the seventh of nine children and from the moment he was born, we all adored him. As a baby, it was so easy to make him smile and giggle, and as he grew, it was not long before he could make all of us kids explode into laughter. He was good natured and mischievous, smart, funny, cheerful and always game. From day one, Danny was a special little kid, and we all knew it.

— Kevin Trant

"Any child can tell you that
the sole purpose of a middle
name is so he can tell when
he's really in trouble."

— DENNIS FAKES

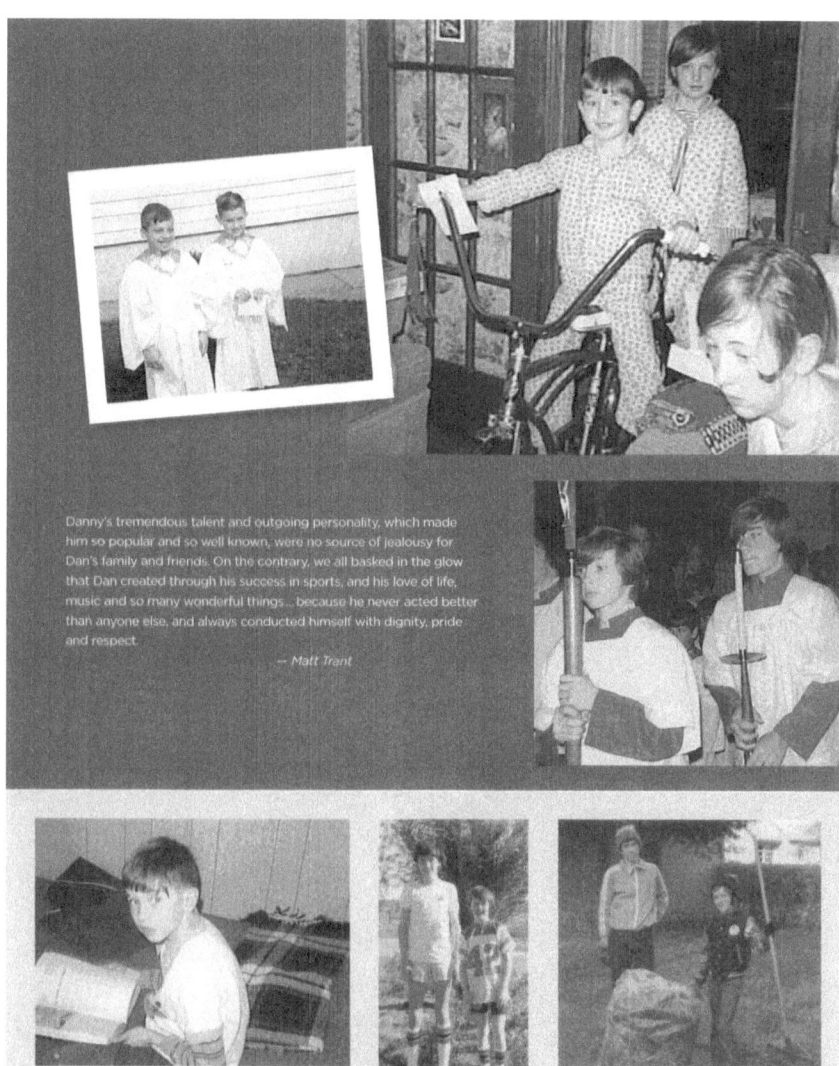

Danny's tremendous talent and outgoing personality, which made him so popular and so well known, were no source of jealousy for Dan's family and friends. On the contrary, we all basked in the glow that Dan created through his success in sports, and his love of life, music and so many wonderful things... because he never acted better than anyone else, and always conducted himself with dignity, pride and respect.

— *Matt Trant*

My father worked with me on my sports skills, how to be a good winner, and a gracious loser. He taught me to be a team player and play within the team concept. He stressed to me, time and again that winning isn't everything. But he also taught me to work hard, and from hard work, you are always a winner.

— *Jessica Trant*
  From a 7th grade essay

Dear Dad,

You died on Tuesday, September 11, 2001.
You were loved by many people and you
loved many people. I remember you as the
best husband, the best Dad, the best influence,
and my best friend.

I know many people are sad that you are gone.
But we can still remember you and see you in
our dreams, our hearts, and in our souls. Right
now, you are saying to all of us, be strong and
I will be there right beside you and guide you
when you have troubles.

We won't be scared, because my Dad is in
Heaven with all good people, and once upon a
time, we will be able to all go to Heaven and be
with you, "Dan The Man".

Love, Daniel
Age 12, September 14, 2001

The best thing about my Dad is that he loves me and he loves his family. He is one of the nicest people I know. He's always there for me and he is always funny. My Dad is really good at sports.

When we went to the Bahamas, my Dad and I slept in the same bed together. We went on a mini cruise on a banana boat. My Dad knows every theme song to every TV show. Whenever we put on a tune, within 5 seconds he knew what TV show it was from and knew all the words to the song.

Whenever I needed help with my schoolwork, my Dad was there to help me. The most special times were when I would go to work with Dad. He would give me whatever I wanted because it was our special time together, the only time we could be alone together.

My Dad went to all my soccer games that he could. He would help me practice at home. Sometimes, I would dress up and it would make Daddy laugh. He liked when I dressed like Britney Spears the best.

I love my Dad and will miss him very much.

— *Alex Trant*
  Age 10, September 14, 2001

*"A life is not important
except in the impact it has
on other lives."*

–JACKIE ROBINSON

To My Brother, Dan Trant:

I'm not sure how many tears I will shed writing this, but I know you deserve to know the affect you had on my life. From high school through college and beyond, you guided me with your knowledge and experiences with your children, you gave me the confidence to be the person I am today. You not only showed my friends and I how to be men, but also, how to raise and care for our future families. We all know how big of sports fans we are in this family. I want to simply explain your impact on my sports world. From the times you came to watch me play baseball and basketball to the times I've played with you and you wouldn't miss a shot for hours. To the times I sat there with my eyes wide open watching videos of your college career and the stories you had almost playing with Bird, McHale, and Parish. Dan, my favorite sports teams are the New York Yankees, New York Giants, New York Rangers, and the Boston Celtics. People say to me, "Boston?" Why Boston? I say—Dan Trant.

Dan, I want to express to you the impact you had on my grandparents life who you probably only met a half dozen times. Every time I would see them, they would ask about that good looking Irish kid your sister married. What a great guy they would say. I know that you were very fond of them as well. It made me feel good to be a part of your family.

From our Cape Cod trip to sipping cocktails around the pool, you always made me feel like your best friend. Dan, you always seemed to impress me more and more each day. I want you to know I have structured my life around you and for that, I am a better person. Dan, I want you to know that I will do anything and everything I can to help your children continue to be the best kids in the world. I know you have the confidence in me to do that, and I will. Dan Trant, you have always been my idol and you will still always be my IDOL!

I Love You,
Your Brother, Chris

City of Westfield

**RICHARD K. SULLIVAN, JR.
MAYOR**

City Hall
59 Court Street
Westfield MA 01085

Telephone: (413) 572-6200
Fax: (413) 572-6274
E-mail: r.sullivan@mail.ci.westfield.ma.us

Dear Trant Family:

It is with a sad heart that I express my personal condolences and those of the citizens of Westfield at the loss of Daniel P. Trant.

I fondly remember Dan as an outstanding basketball player a conscientious employee with the District Attorney's Office and a quality individual.

I will be sure that his name is read at the Community Gathering on the Green this Sunday at 12:00pm, as the City gathers to remember and pray for the victims of the September 11, 2001 terrorist attack, and their families.

We will keep Dan and his family in our prayers and will forward a donation to the children's education fund.

Yours truly,

Richard K. Sullivan, Jr.
Mayor

Jessica Trant   7th Grade

The person who has been my greatest influence in sports is my father. He has taught me everything I know about sports and sportsmanship.

My father started playing sports at a very young age. He told me it takes hard work and discipline to be good at sports. When he was young he would play all sports for hours. When he got into Junior High School he loved soccer and basketball. My father was only 5 feet tall but he never gave up the desire to play sports. He was cut from his Junior High basketball team but did not get discouraged. When he got home from school that day and every day, he went out and practiced until it was dark.

From all his hard work and practice things changed for him in High School. My father played soccer and basketball every year in High School. My father was very good but was still small. He decided to go to Prep School.

He went to Suffield Academy to mature physically and academically and also to be seen by more colleges. He grew to be 6'2" that year. He was team MVP and all New England in basketball and soccer.

My father went to Clark University in Worcester, Mass on a basketball scholarship. He won many individual awards, including being a two-time All American. He was drafted by the Boston Celtics in 1984, and continued playing in Europe for 2 years.

At the age of 5 my father adopted me. At that time, he signed me up for soccer and basketball. My father has been my coach ever since.

My father worked with me on my skills, how to be a good winner, and a gracious loser. He taught me to be a team player and play within the team concept. He stressed to me, time and again that winning isn't everything. But he also taught me to work hard, and from hard work, you are always a winner.

My dad has been an inspiration to me in many different ways when it comes to sports. When I get upset about losing he's there to comfort me. When it comes to understanding sports he's there to explain it to me. When it comes to hugs he's there to hug me. To me he is the greatest inspiration of all.

Senate Resolution No. 225

Offered by Senator Sullivan and Senator Philip, President of the Senate; and Senators Bomke, Bowles, Burzynski, Clayborne, Cronin, Cullerton, DeLeo, del Valle, Demuzio, Dillard, Donahue, Dudycz, Geo-Karis, Halvorson, Hawkinson, Hendon, Jacobs, E. Jones, W. Jones, Karpiel, Klemm, Lauzen, Lightford, Link, Luechtefeld, Madigan, Mahar, Maitland, Molaro, Munoz, Myers, Noland, Obama, O'Daniel, O'Malley, Parker, Peterson, Petka, Radogno, Rauschenberger, Ronen, Roskam, Shadid, Shaw, Sieben, Silverstein, Smith, Stone, Syverson, Trotter, Viverito, L. Walsh, T. Walsh, Watson, Weaver, Welch and Woolard.

WHEREAS, The Members of the Illinois Senate wish to express their sincere condolences to the family and friends of Daniel "Danny" Trant, who passed away on September 11, 2001, at the World Trade Center in New York; and

WHEREAS, In 1991, Mr. Trant moved his family to Long Island, New York, and began a career on Wall Street, working for several brokerage firms before starting at Cantor Fitzgerald in the World Trade Center in 1997; he previously worked for the Hampden County District Attorney's Office in Massachusetts for five years; and

WHEREAS, Mr. Trant loved basketball and was drafted by the Boston Celtics in 1983 but passed up rookie camp to play professional basketball in Ireland; in 1984 and 1985 he played in Cork, Belfast, and Dublin, playing for Jameson, Team Milk, and then leading Team Yoplait in scoring en route to All-Irish National Basketball honors; he returned to the United States to play for the Springfield Fame of the US Basketball League, leading them to a league championship; and

WHEREAS, Mr. Trant was very active as a youth basketball and soccer coach for numerous teams in his church and in his community; and

WHEREAS, The passing of Daniel Trant will be deeply felt by all who knew and loved him, especially his wife, Kathy; his children, Jessica, Daniel, and Alex; his parents; his brothers and sisters; and his many relatives, friends, and colleagues; therefore, be it

RESOLVED, BY THE SENATE OF THE NINETY-SECOND GENERAL ASSEMBLY OF THE STATE OF ILLINOIS, that we mourn, along with all who knew him, the death of Daniel Trant, of Long Island, New York; and be it further

RESOLVED, That suitable copies of this preamble and resolution be presented to the family of Daniel Trant with our sincere condolences.

Adopted by the Senate, November 15, 2001.

_____
President of the Senate

_____
Secretary of the Senate

About the Author

Kathy Trant was born in Staten Island, New York in 1962 and grew up in Massachusetts. She has worked as a legal assistant and bartender, but is most proud of raising three children who are accomplished and kind. Kathy loves travel and adventure, but her goal now is to help people who, like herself, have been through traumatic events. When Ground Zero was being cleared, Kathy was going through her own rebuilding process. She is grateful to have come through it, and did it all for the love of Danny Trant.

www.ingramcontent.com/pod-product-compliance
Lightning Source LLC
Chambersburg PA
CBHW050358290526
45786CB00003B/1039